LETTERS★FROM★THE★HOMEFRONT

WORLD WAR II

VIRGINIA SCHOMP

BENCHMARK BOOKS

MARSHALL CAVENDISH
NEW YORK

Benchmark Books
Marshall Cavendish Corporation
99 White Plains Road
Tarrytown, New York 10591-9001
Website: www.marshallcavendish.com

© Marshall Cavendish Corporation 2002

Library of Congress Cataloging-in-Publication Data
Schomp, Virginia, (date)
World War II / Virginia Schomp.
p. cm. — (Letters from the homefront)
Includes bibliographical references and index.
ISBN 0-7614-1098-8 (lib. bdg.)
1. Soldiers—United States—Correspondence—Juvenile literature. 2. World War, 1939–1945—Personal narratives, American—Juvenile literature. 3. World War, 1939–1945—Press coverage—United States—Juvenile literature. 4. Government and the press—United States—History—20th century—Juvenile literature. [1. World War, 1939–1945—United States. 2. World War, 1939–1945—Personal narratives, American.] I. Title: World War 2. II. Title: World War Two. III. Title. IV. Series
D811.A2 S36   2001   940.54'8173—dc21   00-036038

Book design by Carol Matsuyama
Photo research by Anne Burns Images

Photo Credits
Cover photo: National Archives
The photographs in this book are used by permission and through the courtesy of: *Archive Photos*: 9, 11, 15, 19, 41 (upper left), 83. *The Bancroft Library*: 42. *Corbis*: 21, 37, 41 (upper right), 44, 47, 49, 51, 54, 56, 57, 60, 63, 71, 77. *Franklin D. Roosevelt Library*: 73. *Hulton Getty/Liaison Agency*: 31, 75. *National Archives*: 12, 25, 29, 40, 64, 67. *The Needleman Family*: 26. *U.S. Naval Historical Center*: 17.

ACKNOWLEDGMENTS

With thanks to Glenn C. Altschuler, the Thomas and Dorothy Litwin Professor of American Studies, Cornell University, Ithaca, New York, for his expert reading of the manuscript.

Every effort has been made to trace the copyright holders of letters and other personal writings used in this book. We apologize for any omissions or errors in this regard and would be pleased to make the appropriate acknowledgment in any future printings.

Grateful acknowledgments are made to the following individuals, organizations, and publishers for permission to reprint these materials:

"Ginger's Diary" at http://www.art-bzl.com/diary.html Reprinted by permission of BZ Leonard, site owner.

"Dec. 7 started . . . ," anonymous poem, *Boston Herald*, April 12, 1942. Reprinted by permission of the *Boston Herald*.

Wayne Stutzman to Herbert Raab, October 1, 1942, Raab Family Collection; and Dolores Sampon to J. Donald Peel, March 27, 1943, Sgt. J. Donald Peel Collection, 9th Infantry Division, 5th Army, Box 2. Courtesy of Manuscript Archives, U.S. Army Military History Institute, Carlisle Barracks, Pennsylvania.

Phil Haughey to "Good People," January 31, 1943, Haughey Family Papers, Bentley Historical Library, The University of Michigan. Reprinted by permission of the Bentley Historical Library.

Elsie Rossio and Joseph L. Rauh, Jr., oral histories, from *"The Good War": An Oral History of World War Two*, by Studs Terkel. Reprinted by permission of Donadio & Olson, Inc. Copyright 1984 by Studs Terkel.

Shipyard Diary of a Woman Welder by Augusta Clawson, illustrated by Boris Givotovsky, copyright 1944 by Penguin Books Inc. Used by permission of Viking Penguin, a division of Penguin Putnam Inc.

Polly Crow to William Crow, June 12, 1944; Barbara Sanz to Lester McClannen, June 6, 1944; and Kay McReynolds to Jim McKemy, August 14, 1945. From *Since You Went Away: World War II Letters from American Women on the Home Front*, edited by Judy Barrett Litoff and David C. Smith, copyright 1991 by Judy Barrett Litoff and David C. Smith. Used by permission of Oxford University Press, Inc.

Eleanor Roosevelt to Anna Roosevelt Boettiger, December 31, 1943, Papers of Anna Roosevelt Halsted, box 57, Franklin D. Roosevelt Library, Hyde Park, New York. Courtesy of the Franklin D. Roosevelt Library.

"That Damned Fence," anonymous poem, part of MS 42 United States War Relocation Authority Records. Reprinted by permission of the University of Arizona Library.

Sonoko Iwata to Francis Biddle, July 21, 1942, Snigezo and Sonoko Iwata Papers, the Balch Institute for Ethnic Studies. Reprinted by permission of the Balch Institute for Ethnic Studies.

Elsie Miyata to Esther Pitman, September 19, 1942, "Letters by two Japanese-American school-girls from internment centers during World War II" (Banc MSS 81-43C), the Bancroft Library, University of California, Berkeley. Reprinted by permission of the Bancroft Library.

Louise Ogawa to Clara Breed, November 30, 1942, Gift of Elizabeth Y. Yamada, Japanese American National Museum (93.75.31Q). Reprinted by permission of the Japanese American National Museum.

Joan Dooley to Douglas MacArthur, November 10, 1942. Courtesy of the MacArthur Memorial Archives and Library, Norfolk, Virginia.

Letter to Dunkirk, New York, Rationing Board, from *Americans Remember the Home Front*, by Roy Hoopes, copyright 1977 by Roy Hoopes. Reprinted by permission of Roy Hoopes.

Sammy, Betsy, and David Berman to Reuben Berman, June 7, 1944, September 20, 1944, May 6, 1945, from *Dear Poppa: The World War II Berman Family Letters*, by Ruth Berman, copyright 1997 by the Minnesota Historical Society, letters copyright 1997 by Ruth Berman. Reprinted by permission of Ruth Berman.

Ruth to "Lt.," April 17, 1945. Courtesy of Christina Sharik.

Mrs. N.P. Hansen to John P. Stone, July 19, 1945. Courtesy of the Institute on World War II and the Human Experience, Florida State University, Tallahassee, Florida.

Harry S. Truman to "Mama and Mary," May 8, 1945. Courtesy of the Harry S. Truman Library, Independence, Missouri.

Sincere thanks are also extended to Pam Cheney at the U.S. Army Military History Institute, Carlisle Barracks, Pennsylvania; to the ever-helpful librarians and staff at the E. B. Crawford Library, Monticello, New York; to the eternally patient Lori Wetterer at the Ruth L. Rockwood Memorial Library, Livingston, New Jersey; and to all those who so kindly and generously shared their personal writings and their stories.

CONTENTS

FROM THE AUTHOR

The Letters from the Homefront series got its start in my mother's attic. While rummaging through an old packing trunk stored there, I came across a box of letters written by one of my brothers in 1970–1971, when he served in the army during the Vietnam War. Further searching uncovered a treasure trove of even older family letters, some pasted into scrapbooks, some tucked in shoe boxes, some stacked in tidy bundles tied with faded ribbons. There were notes written by my future grandmother on the eve of World War I and letters from my father describing the B-29 Superfortress bomber he trained in as a tail gunner during World War II. There were cartons filled with fascinating keepsakes: postcards, photos, a food ration book, dusty magazines and record albums, the star banner my mother hung in her front window nearly sixty years ago to show that she had a husband in the service. Each of these items tells a story. Together they offer not only a glimpse into my own family's past but also a snapshot of American life and culture during various times in our nation's history.

Historians often study letters and journals written by famous people—explorers, philosophers, presidents, kings—to gain information about the past. Recently they have discovered the value of writings by "ordinary" people, too. Students of history have begun to seek out and study the letters, diaries, and other personal writings of former slaves and slaveholders, farmers, merchants, foot soldiers, homemakers, and schoolchildren. Documents like these bring a personal voice to history, helping us to understand how older generations lived, worked, and played, and how historical events shaped their lives.

A number of libraries, cultural societies, and museums have

put special effort into locating and preserving personal documents from the World War II era. Recognizing the value of papers from those momentous times, some people have donated their old family letters to libraries, while others have published them in books or posted them on personal websites. Historians have put together collections of letters and remembrances by Americans who served in World War II as well as those who lived through the turbulent war years on the homefront—the people journalist Tom Brokaw has called the "Greatest Generation." The members of that generation played a major role in building the world we live in today. This book tells their story, in their own words, and through them seeks to understand how World War II challenged, inspired, and transformed American society.

INTRODUCTION: THE ROAD TO WAR

The "war to end all wars." That was the name given to World War I, the terrible conflict that raged from 1914 to 1918, killing more than ten million people. World War I grew out of disputes among the European nations over control of territories in Europe, Africa, and Asia. Two great alliances formed: on one side were the Allies (mainly France, Great Britain, Italy, Russia, and the United States), and on the other were the Central Powers (Germany, Austria-Hungary, and Turkey). The Allies defeated the Central Powers, and the bloody war ended with the signing of a peace treaty at Versailles, France.

Under the terms of the Versailles treaty, Germany suffered especially harsh punishments. Its economic hardships multiplied in 1929, with the beginning of the worldwide Great Depression. Hungry and desperate, still angry over the humiliating Versailles settlement, the German people turned to a rising young politician who promised to restore their nation to greatness—Adolf Hitler. Hitler and his followers in the Nazi Party built a new German government, a dictatorship based on fear, violence, and hatred, especially of the Jews. In 1939 the Nazi leader set out to bring the rest of Europe under his control.

Hitler was not alone in his dreams of power. Italy's Fascist Party leader, Benito Mussolini, had seized control of his country's government and launched wars of conquest against Ethiopia and Albania. Japan's military leaders, eager to establish an Asian empire, had invaded China. In 1940 Germany, Italy, and Japan united forces by signing the Tripartite Pact. Together they would be known as the Axis powers.

While the world marched toward war, the United States,

DICTATORS ADOLF
HITLER OF GERMANY
AND BENITO MUSSOLINI
OF ITALY USED BRUTE
FORCE AND TERROR TO
PURSUE DREAMS OF
POWER AND GLORY.

remembering that World War I had not succeeded in creating a lasting peace, remained neutral. Americans watched with growing concern as the Nazi blitzkrieg ("lightning war") swallowed up Poland, Norway, Denmark, Belgium, the Netherlands, and France. They supported President Franklin D. Roosevelt's plan to send aid to Great Britain in that country's lonely, desperate fight against Hitler's forces. They condemned Japan's aggression in China. Some even argued that U.S. military forces should help the countries fighting for democracy. But most Americans wanted their country to stay out of foreign wars.

December 7, 1941, changed all that. Japan's surprise attack on the U.S. naval base at Pearl Harbor shocked and enraged the nation. Disagreements were forgotten. Suddenly Americans were united in their commitment to total war against the Axis powers. It was a war that would shake the world and change the face of America forever.

1

ARSENAL OF DEMOCRACY

Dec. 7 started like any other quiet Sunday in Hawaii . . .
Then things began to happen.
We heard the rumble of guns firing.
There were black airplanes in the sky. . . .
The telephone rang.
My father answered.
He was called to his destroyer because the Japanese
were attacking Pearl Harbor.
We could stand on the porch and see some of the fighting.
It looked like a Fourth of July celebration.

—STEPHANIE CARLSON, AGE TEN

America Goes to War

The bombs were still falling when most Americans got the news: "We interrupt this program to bring you a special news bulletin. The Japanese have attacked Pearl Harbor." In a surprise raid at dawn, a massive assault force of Japanese bombers and fighter planes had attacked the U.S. naval base at Pearl Harbor on the Hawaiian island of Oahu. It was the worst military disaster in American history. Eighteen ships were sunk or badly damaged, nearly two hundred planes were destroyed, and more than 2,400 people were killed. Within hours the Japanese also attacked other airfields on Oahu as well as targets in the Philippines, Singapore,

THE USS *MARYLAND*
BATTLESHIP GOES DOWN
IN FLAMES DURING THE
JAPANESE ATTACK ON
PEARL HARBOR.

Pearl Harbor in Flames

Ginger Bailey lived at Hickam Field, Oahu, Hawaii, at the time of the Japanese bombing on December 7, 1941. The seventeen-year-old high school senior recorded the events of that fateful day in her diary.

BOMBED! 8:00 in the morning. Unknown attacker so far! Pearl Harbor in flames! Also Hickam hangar line. So far no houses bombed here.

5 of 11:00. We've left the post. It got too hot. The PX is in flames, also the barracks. We made a dash during a lull. Left everything we own there. Found out the attackers are Japs. Rats!!! A couple of non-coms' houses demolished. Hope Kay is O.K. We're at M's. It's all so sudden and surprising I can't believe it's really happening. It's awful. School is discontinued until further notice . . . there goes my graduation.

Shortwave: Direct hit on barracks, 350 killed. Wonder if I knew any of them. Been quiet all afternoon. Left Bill [Ginger's older brother] on duty at the U [University of Hawaii]. Blackout all night of course!

LET'S GO!

U·S·MARINES

RECRUITING POSTERS URGED PATRIOTIC AMERICANS TO JOIN THE NATION'S FIGHT.

Malaya, and Hong Kong. In one stroke Japan had gained control of the skies and seas across one-quarter of the earth.

Americans reacted with shock and outrage. In some cases they panicked. On the West Coast—the area closest to the invaders— searchlights combed the skies and antiaircraft guns blasted at imaginary warplanes. Ragtag "armies" bearing clubs, pistols, and squirrel guns patrolled the beaches, on the watch for enemy landing parties. The roofs of government buildings in Washington, D.C., bristled with machine guns. President Roosevelt did say no to one proposal from the army—to paint the White House black.

The hysteria quickly died down. In its place Americans united in a surge of patriotism and steely purpose. "First it was indignation, then it turned to anger," a Michigan man recalls, "and by the time one went to work the following morning it was determination: 'They can't do that to us.'" Thousands of young men flocked to army and navy recruiting stations. Many more were drafted. By war's end some sixteen million men and women would wear a uniform.

WHEN THE UNITED STATES ENTERED WORLD WAR II, ONLY MEN AGED TWENTY-ONE TO THIRTY-FIVE COULD BE DRAFTED, BUT YOUNGER AND OLDER MEN COULD ENLIST ON THEIR OWN. MANY LEAPED AT THE CHANCE. SIXTEEN-YEAR-OLD WAYNE STUTZMAN SHARED HIS IMPATIENCE WITH HIS FORMER SCHOOLTEACHER, HERBERT RAAB, AN ENLISTED MAN SERVING WITH THE 301ST ENGINEERING BATTALION IN ITALY.

Johnstown, Pa.
October 1, 1942

Dear Mr. Raab

All the rest of the pupils in our class are writing letters to you and I know what they are going to say so I'll try to say something different. And to be honest with you I've spent half of bookkeeping class thinking of what to say and this is how much I thought of. Mr. McIlany threatened to kick me out of class if I didn't quit saying over and over to myself, "Dear Mr. Raab," "Dear Mr. Raab," "Dear Mr. Raab."

School is the same old drag for me except for a few changes in the schedule. In many ways the school is worse than ever before. The hours are longer, the teachers are getting older, and we don't have your warm smile and cheery "hello" to keep room 202 as pleasant as it was when it was in your hands.

I hope your new life in the army is not as bad as some people say it is. I know it is hard for a person to leave his home and family but when you know it is one way of helping to win freedom it seems to make it easier. . . .

Many men and boys have already left this area since Dec. 7 and many more will be going in the near future. There are many boys like myself who are "raring to go". On November 18, I will be 17 years old. As you know that is the minimum age for boys in the navy. Well on that date I intend going down to enlist. If they accept me I'll be in that branch of the service fighting to keep America a country where the pupils don't have to salute their teachers.

Former student and friend,
Wayne Stutzman

While GIs—named for their "Government Issue" uniforms—served on battlefronts around the world, millions of other Americans did their part at home. They worked in defense factories, volunteered for civil defense, sacrificed comforts and conveniences, and kept up the GIs' spirits with an endless avalanche of mail. These Americans were part of the dynamic wartime world that historians call the homefront. This book tells their story, in their own words, as recorded in their letters, diaries, and personal reflections on the war years.

Miracles of Production

No matter how eager and confident its citizens might be, the United States was not prepared for war. As Hitler's armies marched across Europe, Americans were still struggling to recover from the Great Depression. That economic crisis, which began with the stock market crash of 1929, had closed countless banks and businesses and put sixteen million people out of work. A year before Pearl Harbor, President Roosevelt had ordered increased government spending on military weapons and supplies, determined to transform the nation into the "great arsenal [weapons maker] of democracy." Still, the first American troops of World War II had to train with make-believe wooden rifles and drive Ford trucks hung with cardboard signs identifying them as "tanks."

"Speed and speed now" was Roosevelt's call. And after Pearl Harbor industry responded with an almost miraculous flood of war materials. New factories were built, older ones expanded. Factories that had been making civilian goods converted to "defense plants." Vacuum cleaner manufacturers turned out machine guns. Automakers built tanks and airplanes. A soft drinks company, experienced in filling bottles with liquids, began filling shell casings with explosives. The sudden boom in production created millions of new jobs.

MILLIONS OF AMERICANS WENT TO WORK AT DEFENSE FACTORIES, CHURNING OUT AN AVALANCHE OF PLANES, TANKS, AND OTHER WAR MATERIALS.

"After all those years of the Depression when men had to sit around without work," one woman recalls, "it was kind of exciting just to see the rows of men going off to work at the plants with lunch pails under their arms." War eliminated unemployment practically overnight. Anyone who wanted a job could find one. Even people who weren't necessarily looking for work sometimes found themselves part of the war effort: police in some cities rounded up stragglers hanging out on street corners and hauled them to the local employment office to look over the job listings.

WITH MILLIONS OF AMERICANS SERVING OVERSEAS, FACTORIES STRUGGLED TO MEET PRODUCTION DEMANDS. PHIL HAUGHEY, CHIEF DRAFTSMAN AT A SHIPYARD NEAR PORTLAND, OREGON, WROTE TO HIS PARENTS IN MICHIGAN ABOUT THE CHALLENGES OF PRODUCING MORE AND MORE WITH FEWER AND FEWER HANDS. PHIL'S MOTHER, EDITH, HELPED HER EIGHT GROWN CHILDREN KEEP IN TOUCH DURING THE WAR BY TYPING OUT ALL THE LETTERS THEY SENT HOME AND MAILING CARBON COPIES TO EACH.

Sunday Jan 31 [1943]

Dear Good People—

Another Sunday has rolled around, and it seems to be my standard day for letter writing. And by the way, Mother, your typing looks very professional now. Surprising, isn't it, what practice will do.

Things at the office are rolling along pretty well. We are still working 60 hours a week which is pretty tough. Clif [Phil's brother, the naval architect in charge of the shipyard] has big worries like whether or not to spend $200,000 on an extension of the ways in order to launch this larger ship etc. I have what to me are big worries, like how to turn the work out when the army keeps grabbing our men. Funny thing about this army stuff. If they had an informer right in our office they couldn't pick better men than they have grabbed with the draft. We start with mostly raw kids and teach them what we want them to know. The smart ones, the ones who catch on are invariably [constantly] hustled away from us. In Jan. we lost 2. In February we are to lose 3 more. This should be a hell of a fine army if the boys they have taken from us are representative.

Friday I had an interesting day. With three other men from the yard I went on the trial trip of an aircraft carrier. This ship, the "H.M.S. TRACKER" is a merchant ship, converted into a carrier. . . . Carriers are pretty new to Portland, and this one had a very fancy job of camouflage. To put it mildly the ship was a sensation to whoever saw her, and there were cheers and blasts of greeting from all who had a chance to hail us. . . .

We are eating regularly. We don't have as much of some items as we would have in other times, but we make adjustments. The days of the steak roasts at the lake though, seem lost in a haze of memory. . . .

Love to you all,
Phil

Americans were proud of their role as defense workers. Don Johnson, who worked on bomber parts at a General Motors plant in Michigan, recalls that Pearl Harbor caused

an immediate change in people's attitude toward their work— their sense of urgency, their dedication, their team work. When the chips were down, people dealt with it like survival. Things that might have taken days longer were done to meet a target so you didn't hold somebody else up—even if it meant putting in extra hours and extra effort.

High production goals often did call for extra effort. Most factories operated twenty-four hours a day, seven days a week, with employees putting in fifty or even sixty hours a week. Workers punching in at dawn passed tired coworkers just heading home from the "graveyard" shift. Those with a loved one in the service felt

FACTORIES STRUGGLING TO MEET HIGH PRODUCTION GOALS OFTEN RELIED ON THE SKILLS OF NEWLY HIRED WOMEN WORKERS.

a special responsibility. They liked to tell the story of a seaman named Elgin Staples, whose ship had gone down in the Pacific. It turned out that the life preserver Elgin was wearing when rescued had been packed and inspected by his own mother back in Ohio.

Remarkable results came out of this round-the-clock hum of activity. West Coast shipyards launched two ten-thousand-ton cargo carriers a day, and one Michigan aircraft plant turned out one B-24 Liberator bomber every sixty-three minutes. By the time World War II ended, American factories and shipyards had produced more planes, ships, tanks, weapons, ammunition, and other war materials than the rest of the world combined. These miracles of production helped win the war. They also brought new prosperity to an American workforce that was on the move like never before.

A Nation in Motion

More than thirty million Americans—one-fifth of the country's population—left home during World War II. Half were GIs bound for training camps or assignments overseas. Half were civilians— ordinary men, women, and children swept up in the largest and most dramatic mass movement in American history.

"Ford Builds New Plant." That kind of headline spelled opportunity for Americans just emerging from the hard times of the Great Depression. Millions of people eagerly pulled up stakes and headed for jobs at the new defense plants. Many left mountain towns and farms for jobs in the cities. Some traveled to oil fields in the south or to manufacturing complexes in the east or the Great Lakes region. A million and a half African Americans left the south, many for jobs in northern cities. But the largest wave of migrants headed west, to the booming shipyards and aircraft plants along the Pacific coast.

Another group of wartime migrants were "camp followers"—

ASSEMBLY LINES MADE
IT POSSIBLE FOR
FACTORIES TO MASS-
PRODUCE PLANES AND
OTHER WAR MATERIALS
AT RECORD SPEED.

wives and children who moved with servicemen from one military base to another. Moving was hard on mothers with young children. "We didn't fly. It was always a train," a California woman remembers. "No place to sleep, sit up maybe three, four nights. The trains were filthy, crowded. . . . Women . . . traveling with small children. Trying to feed their kids, diaper their kids." For many older children the hardest part was having to change schools, sometimes two or three times in a single year. "I was *always* the new kid in the classroom," one woman recalls, "the one who didn't stay long enough to make any friends." With all its difficulties this restless lifestyle was the only way for desperate couples to keep their families together as long as possible, until the day the GI was shipped overseas.

Camp followers and defense workers shared a common problem: the nation's sudden and severe housing shortage. As America's

Mail Call

I need a lot of mail. That is all a fellow has to look forward to—is mail call. That's all there is to keep a guy's morale [spirits] up or give him any morale at all. So, please, do write me a lot for you are all I have, and I do like to hear from you, really I do.

Charles Taylor's plea to his young wife, Barbara, echoed the feelings of thousands of other American GIs serving far from home. The bugle call to mail distribution was one of the most important and most anticipated parts of the soldier's life. "Letters were a big part of our emotional stability," one World War II veteran recalls, "because they made us feel like we were still a part of the people back home, that we hadn't been forgotten."

Through fast and efficient mail delivery, Americans on the homefront were able to keep in closer contact with servicemen and women than had been possible in any previous war. The volume of mail was amazing. In 1945 alone Americans sent 3½ billion pieces of mail overseas. Much of this was Victory Mail, or V-Mail. V-Mail letters were typed on special 8½-by-11-inch paper, which the government reduced to microfilm size for shipment, then enlarged to a 4-by-5½-inch photograph for reading. V-Mail saved cargo space needed for the shipment of war materials—2,575 pounds of mail could be reduced to just 45 pounds.

Wartime letters reflected the many concerns of homefront Americans. They were filled with love, fear, loneliness, and news of work, shortages, rationing, and the other challenges of the times. Many wives wrote their husbands every day and encouraged even young children to scribble a few lines to "Daddy." Letters were a way for children to keep in touch with a father who often seemed little more than a photograph on the mantle or a half-forgotten dream.

A LETTER FROM HOME BRINGS A BIG SMILE TO THIS SERVICEMAN'S FACE.

population reshuffled, towns saw their numbers soar. Thousands of people arriving at areas near military installations, factories, and shipyards scrambled for the few available houses and apartments. Many newcomers had to crowd into bare rooms, abandoned garages, tent cities, and trailer camps as small towns became "boomtowns" overnight.

S ENECA, ILLINOIS, WAS A SLEEPY COUNTRY TOWN ON THE ILLINOIS RIVER, SEVENTY MILES SOUTHWEST OF CHICAGO. DURING THE WAR A NEW SHIPYARD TURNED SENECA INTO A BOOMTOWN. ELSIE ROSSIO REMEMBERS THE COMMOTION AND EXCITEMENT OF THOSE TIMES.

Around late 1940, we began hearing rumors that the government was going to build a shipyard here. The men who did not have work were excited. We were still feeling the Depression. The trucks began rolling in with great loads of material. In my lifetime, we never had this traffic. Then came the new people, cars and cars and cars.

You'd hear the rat-a-tat-tat of hammering all night long. The traffic seemed to be going on all night, too. Even the dogs knew enough to hide. You didn't see them running across the street any more. People didn't stand on the street and visit like they used to.

At the time we were only about a thousand people. One restaurant, an old hotel, that was all. All of a sudden Seneca and the surrounding area had about 27,000. You would wake up in the morning and someone would be rolled up in a blanket on your front porch. Everybody took in boarders. Then the government built barracks and new housing for the workers.

The merchants did very well. It was so crowded that we had to stand in line the longest time with our ration books and food stamps. We weren't used to this. On the whole, the feeling toward the new people was good, although there was some resentment here and there. Many came from the South and we heard all sorts of strange accents.

The most famous boomtown was Willow Run, Michigan, site of a giant Ford aircraft plant. Before the war about 16,000 people lived in Willow Run; by the end of 1942 the area had 32,000 new residents. Until Ford built temporary housing units, many of these workers jammed into a trailer camp where outhouses leaked into the drinking water and disease and fire constantly threatened.

"Before the bomber plant was built, everything was perfect here," one Willow Run old-timer complained. "Then came that bomber plant and this influx of riffraff. . . . You can't be sure of these people." Local residents often resented the noise, congestion, and confusion brought by newcomers. "You never got the feeling that you were welcome," says Dellie Hahne, who traveled with her GI husband to army bases in Florida and Texas. "I was an outsider. . . . We were looked down upon." One reporter looking into conditions in boomtowns was told, "Folks in houses think trailer people are vermin."

Despite all the hardships most wartime migrants found what they were looking for: a steady job and good money. Defense plant jobs paid well, especially with overtime bonuses added in. For the first time in years, families had money to save and to spend. Most believed they had made the right decision in migrating. In fact, millions of Americans who had moved during the war years never returned home. War had opened up new opportunities for American workers, including many who had never had a chance to share in the nation's wealth before.

2

ROSIE THE RIVETER

Suddenly I saw something I hadn't seen before. My sister became Rosie the Riveter. She put a bandanna on her head every day and went down to this organ company that had been converted to war work. There was my sister in slacks. It became more than work. There was a sense of mission about it. Her husband was Over There.

—MIKE ROYKO, A CHICAGO RESIDENT

Women War Workers

"If you can drive a car you can run a machine." That was the slogan adopted by one defense plant trying to attract women workers. Production was booming. Men were marching off to war. Women were needed to fill all those jobs at shipyards and factory assembly lines.

Many women already worked outside the home. At the beginning of World War II, women made up 25 percent of the American labor force. By 1944 that figure had jumped to 36 percent, with five million women answering industry's call to "enlist" at their local employment office. The numbers were impressive. But even more exciting were the kinds of jobs these workers found—jobs that had never been open to women before.

"When the war started I was twenty-six, unmarried, and working as a cosmetics clerk in a drugstore," Adele Erenberg remembers. Quitting her old job, Adele went to work in the machine shop at an

AMERICAN WOMEN WERE INSPIRED BY "ROSIE THE RIVETER," THE HARDY HEROINE OF GOVERNMENT AD CAMPAIGNS ENCOURAGING WOMEN TO TAKE A DEFENSE JOB.

WOMEN ON ASSEMBLY LINES OFTEN SHARED A SPECIAL SENSE OF COOPERATION AND COMRADESHIP—A SPIRIT CAPTURED IN PHOTOS AND IN THIS ILLUSTRATION BY EDNA COHEN, A FACTORY WORKER IN BROOKLYN, N.Y.

aircraft plant. "For me defense work was the beginning of my emancipation [becoming free] as a woman," she says. "For the first time in my life I found out that I could do something with my hands besides bake a pie." Millions of other salesclerks, secretaries, cooks, maids, and waitresses moved on to what had always been considered "men's work." They became cab drivers, mail carriers, and elevator operators. They pumped gas, wrote for newspapers and radio stations, played in symphony orchestras, and worked for the government and stock market. Most women, though, worked in manufacturing, especially in the defense industries.

AUGUSTA CLAWSON KEPT A DIARY OF HER EXPERIENCES AS A SHIPYARD WELDER DURING THE WAR. WELDERS JOIN METAL PARTS BY HEATING THEM AND LETTING THE MELTED METALS BLEND TOGETHER. IT'S A DIFFICULT JOB THAT FORMERLY HAD BEEN DONE ONLY BY MEN. AUGUSTA'S WRITINGS TRACE HER PROGRESS FROM FIRST-DAY JITTERS TO PRIDE IN HER GROWING STRENGTH AND SKILLS.

Wednesday, *April 7 [1943]:*

Well, I've done it! I've joined the ranks of war workers—I'm going to be a welder in The Shipyard. It was a sudden decision, and I'm proud of it— I think. But right now, this minute, though I hate to admit it, I'm a bit panicky. It's been an interesting day but a terrifying one in a strange intangible [not clearly felt] way. There is a nervous, or perhaps it's an emotional, strain about a day like this. It must be the natural apprehension [fear] one feels on entering anything new and unknown. . . .

Wednesday *[April 14]:*

I have completed six days of training, and tonight am the proud owner of two things: one—a black metal lunchbox complete with thermos; two—a firm conviction that I shall become a welder. I've had a few doubts about the latter, wondered sometimes if I could take it. No—that's exaggerated. I knew I would be a welder because I'd made up my mind, and I was going to do it or else. . . . But it was mostly a resolve, until now. Tonight I'm sure, because I'm getting such a kick out of it, and because I can see progress. . . .

Friday *[April 16]:*

. . . I am today the proud owner of one check drawn by The Shipyard and payable to one A. H. Clawson, Badge 44651—$20.80 for the three days of last week. I'll have to pay [most of] it over to Uncle Sam [in taxes], but it's fun having it even go through my hands. And I shall keep the stub as a record for posterity [future generations]. I must have a grandchild, even if I have to adopt one, so that I can say, "Darling, in the last war your grandmother built ships." (Probably by then my granddaughter will be an Admiral and won't be impressed at all.)

Tuesday *[April 20]*:

. . . My muscles have been forced to develop and harden so rapidly . . . that they are like a watch spring that is wound too tight; they seem to be ready to burst through the skin. It's a queer sensation. You can certainly feel the wheels go round in this hardening-up process.

And it isn't only your muscles that must harden. It's your nerve, too. I admit quite frankly that I was scared pink when I had to climb on top deck today. It's as if you had to climb from the edge of the fifth story up to the sixth of a house whose outside walls have not been put on. Even the scaffolding around the side is not very reassuring, for there are gaps between, where you are sure you'll fall through. The men know their muscles are strong enough to pull them up if they get a firm grip on a bar above. But we women do not yet trust our strength, and some of us do not like heights. But one does what one has to. And it's surprising what one can do when it's necessary. . . .

Monday *[April 26]*:

I have completed seven days of work in the Shipyard, and something has happened. I don't quite know what it is, but after work today I suddenly realized that I had no dread or fear any more in connection with this job. I feel like an emancipated welder.

When nine-year-old Mike Royko's older sister took a war job, he thought of the attractive poster girl in work overalls who proudly showed off her bulging muscles and urged women, "We Can Do It!" Rosie the Riveter was an imaginary figure used in ad campaigns. But she was also a reality. During the war millions of women served as riveters (airplane assemblers), welders, mechanics, steelworkers, crane operators—almost any defense job that needed doing.

Many of these women went to work out of patriotism—to do something for the war effort. Those with husbands and sons in the service found that work helped pass the long hours of worry and loneliness. And most had another very practical reason for working:

with the family "breadwinner" away at war, they needed the money.

Defense jobs paid much better than the kinds of work women had done before. Performing difficult, vital labor also gave these workers a new sense of independence and self-confidence. But there were frustrations, too. Women's pay was good, but men's was better. Even when they did the same jobs as men, women earned about 40 percent less. They had to put up with sneers and hostility from male coworkers who believed that a woman's place was in the home.

MECHANICS REPAIR AN AIRCRAFT ENGINE AT A JACKSONVILLE, FLORIDA, NAVAL AIR STATION.

When Adele Erenberg started in the machine shop, she found that "it took . . . two weeks before anyone even talked to me. The discrimination was indescribable. They wanted to kill me." Frankie Cooper operated a fifty-ton crane at an Illinois steel mill. "The men said, 'It's too big a responsibility for a woman. She'll never last,' " Frankie recalls. "After that I had to. I had to show them I could do it."

Women in Uniform

On May 27, 1942, the U.S. Army opened its recruiting stations to women for the first time. The response was overwhelming. In some cities women stood in line for more than eight hours to sign up. At least one center ran out of application forms. Altogether, 143,000 women would serve their country in the WAC (Women's Army Corps). Another 200,000 would join the WAVES (the navy's Women Accepted for Volunteer Emergency Service), WASP (Women Airforce Service Pilots), Army and Navy Nurse Corps, and women's reserves of the Marine Corps and Coast Guard. These women volunteers did hundreds of different jobs. They served as clerks and switchboard operators, analyzed enemy codes, repaired and drove trucks, tested aircraft, and ferried planes to military bases. Their contributions freed up thousands of servicemen for combat duty.

Many civilians and GIs treated women in uniform like second-class citizen-soldiers. "Goddam it all, first they send us dogs. Now it's women," one Marine Corps officer exploded when the first female recruits arrived. A soldier trying to persuade his sister not to enlist wrote, "Why can't these gals just stay home and be their own sweet self." Attitudes such as these only inspired women to train and work harder. By performing their duties capably, they made a valuable contribution to the armed services and paved the way for future women in the military.

MORE THAN 100,000 WOMEN VOLUNTEERED TO
SERVE IN THE WAVES, THE SPECIAL ALL-FEMALE
BRANCH OF THE U.S. NAVY.

Like a lot of working women, Frankie had an added responsibility: a two-year-old daughter. Many women who worked forty or fifty hours a week also bore the full burden of caring for their children and tending to household chores such as cooking, cleaning, sewing, and shopping. There were few day care centers. While they worked, mothers usually left young children in the care of a relative, neighbor, or older brother or sister. And they worried. "Leaving my . . . daughter [was the] one really difficult problem with working," Frankie Cooper recalls. "When a mother goes away from home and starts to work for her first time, there is always a feeling of guilt." It didn't help when some religious and political leaders criticized working mothers for "abandoning" their children. These "neglected" children, warned FBI Director J. Edgar Hoover, were in danger of "stumbling into the dreaded maze of delinquency and disease, of reformatory and prison, or, if they are not apprehended [captured], of maiming and plundering."

In reality, nearly all women managed to juggle their many responsibilities and make sure their children were safe, happy, and well cared for. When the war ended, most Americans agreed that the battle could not have been won without the contributions of women war workers.

Women Alone

Even with all their contributions in the workforce, most women still put marriage and family first. There were more marriages in 1942 than ever before in U.S. history, and in 1943 jewelers warned that the supply of wedding rings had reached an all-time low. Some wartime marriages were simply a sign of the new prosperity—couples who had put off marriage during the Great Depression finally had the cash to live out their dreams. Many other marriages reflected the uncertainties and emotions stirred up by war.

"It was . . . a very hectic, exciting time, but there was always an underlying sadness," remembers one California woman. "Relationships were extremely intense, because you didn't know how long

ALONG WITH HER INFANT SON, BILL, POLLY CROW MOVED IN WITH HER MOTHER AFTER HER HUSBAND, WILLIAM, WAS SENT TO FIGHT IN EUROPE. IN A LETTER TO WILLIAM ABOUT HER NEW JOB AT A SHIPYARD, POLLY TOUCHED ON SOME OF THE JOYS AND CHALLENGES OF BECOMING A WORKING MOTHER.

Louisville, June 12, 1944

Darlin':

You are now the husband of a career woman—just call me your little Ship Yard Babe! Yeh! I made up my mind that I wanted to work from 4:00 P.M. 'till midnight so's I could have my cake and eat it too. I wanted to work but didn't want to leave Bill all day—in the first place it would be too much for Mother altho' she was perfectly willing and then Bill needs me. This way Mother will just have to feed him once and tuck him in which is no trouble at all any more as I just put him in bed and let him play quietly until he's ready to go to sleep and he drops right off. . . . I finally ended up with just what I wanted. Comptometer [calculator] job—4:00 'till midnite—70 cents an hour to start which amounts to $36.40 a week, $145.60 per month, increase in two months if I'm any good and I know I will be. Oh yeh! At Jeffersonville Boat and Machine Co. I'll have to go over to Jeffersonville, Ind. which will take about 45 minutes each way. Hope I can get a ride home each nite as that's the only feature I dislike but I'm not gonna be a sissy. If I can't get a ride, I'll get tags for our buggy and probably use it. . . . If I don't need it for work I may not get them but will just have to see how things work out. Want to take Bill out swimming a lot this summer so I may need it for that. . . .

Opened my little checking account too and it's a grand and glorious feeling to write a check all your own and not have to ask for one. Any hoo, I don't want it said I charged things to 'em and didn't pay it so we don't owe anybody anything and I'm gonna start sockin' it in the savings and checking too so's we'll have something when our sweet little Daddy comes home.

Good nite, Darlin'
I love you, Polly

Allotment Annies

Scheming women who married servicemen solely for their $50 monthly government allotment check and $10,000 life insurance policy were known as Allotment Annies. Seventeen-year-old Elvira Tayloe lived near a large naval base in Norfolk, Virginia. Elvira was married to six sailors and was working on her seventh when two of her husbands met by accident in an English pub. After trading photographs—and punches—the two men joined forces, alerted authorities, and ended the career of this particular "Annie."

they would last." Frances Veeder, who was seventeen when the war began, explains that

> there were many, like myself, who got caught up in the war fever. . . . There was a kind of fierceness, almost a desperation, about people meeting each other at that time. It might sound corny, but there was that attitude of "Well, I'm going to be shipping out next week, so let's stay up all night and dance."

Some couples jumped into marriage after only a few brief dates. Others were longtime sweethearts who rushed to the altar when the man received his orders to ship overseas. Life was hard for the "war brides." Young and inexperienced, they had to cope with loneliness, fears of loss, and, in many cases, the challenges of earning a living and caring for a new baby on their own. "Georgie keeps me busy and takes my mind off you sometimes," Catherine Young wrote to her GI husband a month after their son's birth; "still I miss you just as much if not more than ever. . . . Come back to us, Darling." Marjorie Cartwright, who moved to San Francisco to be near her navy husband's home port, recalls, "I lived alone for four years during the war, and they were the most painful, lonely years I think I will ever spend."

Some wartime marriages could not bear the strain. In 1945 about a half million couples were divorced—almost double the number in 1940. But most couples managed to keep their love alive. Men fought and dreamed of home. And on the homefront wives and sweethearts worked and hoped and waited.

FIRST LADY ELEANOR ROOSEVELT OFTEN LEFT SPECIAL PERSONAL NOTES TO FAMILY MEMBERS ON THEIR PILLOWS, TO BE FOUND AND READ AT BEDTIME. SHE LEFT THIS NOTE—EVIDENCE OF HER UNDERSTANDING AND COMPASSION FOR THE UNHAPPINESS OF WAR WIVES—TO HER DAUGHTER, ANNA, ON NEW YEAR'S EVE 1943. ANNA'S HUSBAND, JOHN BOETTIGER, WAS AN ARMY CAPTAIN SERVING IN EUROPE.

New Year's Eve

Anna darling,

This is just a little line for you to carry with you thro' the coming year.
I know how empty life seems, how purposeless & how deeply lonely. The contrast between great companionship & the present blank is what makes it so hard to bear.
I can hope & pray that the coming year will bring your John back & you know that both of you are never out of my mind & heart. God bless & keep you both & give you health & strength for this ordeal.
All my love, admiration & devotion to you dearest one.

Mother

DEMOCRACY DENIED

They've sunk the posts deep into the ground
They've strung out wires all the way around.
With machine gun nests just over there,
And sentries and soldiers everywhere.

We're trapped like rats in a wired cage,
To fret and fume with impotent [helpless] rage;
Yonder whispers the lure of the night,
But that DAMNED FENCE assails our sight. . . .

We all love life, and our country best,
Our misfortune to be here in the west,
To keep us penned behind that DAMNED FENCE,
Is someone's notion of NATIONAL DEFENCE!

—ANONYMOUS POEM CIRCULATED AT THE POSTON,
ARIZONA, JAPANESE-AMERICAN INTERNMENT CAMP

A "Grave Injustice"

"Open season on 'Japs'—no license required," proclaimed an official at the Tennessee Department of Hunting Licenses. A violent hatred of the Japanese spread across the United States like a fever during the early months of World War II. Hostile signs appeared in restaurants and store windows: "No Dogs or Japs Allowed."

One California barbershop offered "free shaves for Japs" but was "not responsible for accidents."

At the time of Pearl Harbor, some 127,000 people of Japanese heritage lived in the United States, almost all on the West Coast. About one-third were Issei—immigrants born in Japan. The rest were Japanese Americans, born in the United States and therefore American citizens.

Japanese Americans had long been the target of prejudice and discrimination. After Pearl Harbor the hatred multiplied. Wild

MANY CALIFORNIANS HUNG SIGNS ON THEIR HOMES AND BUSINESSES TO FORCE THE JAPANESE FROM THEIR COMMUNITIES.

rumors spread: "Jap" fishermen were planting mines in Pacific harbors; farmers were stuffing vegetables with arsenic to send to market; families living near a California naval base were spies plotting an invasion. Though there was no truth behind any of these stories, citizens and business groups, journalists and politicians began to clamor for the removal of all Japanese from the area.

On February 19, 1942, President Roosevelt signed Executive Order 9066, authorizing the forcible evacuation from the West Coast of all people of Japanese heritage, citizens and noncitizens alike. Families had forty-eight hours to get ready. They could bring only what they could carry. The rest—businesses, farms, homes, personal possessions—had to be abandoned, stored, or sold at cut-rate prices to bargain hunters.

DURING THE JAPANESE EVACUATIONS, TWO THOUSAND MEN WERE SEPARATED FROM THEIR FAMILIES AND IMPRISONED IN SPECIAL CAMPS SET ASIDE FOR "SUSPICIOUS ENEMY ALIENS [NONCITIZENS]." ALL OF THESE MEN WERE ISSEI—JAPANESE IMMIGRANTS WHO, UNDER U.S. LAW, HAD NEVER BEEN ALLOWED TO APPLY FOR AMERICAN CITIZENSHIP. MOST WERE CONSIDERED "DANGEROUS" BECAUSE THEY BELONGED TO SOME JAPANESE CULTURAL OR BUSINESS ORGANIZATION. SHIGEZO IWATA, AN OFFICIAL WITH A FARMERS' TRADE ASSOCIATION, SPENT A YEAR IN ONE OF THE SEPARATE CAMPS BEFORE LETTERS OF APPEAL WRITTEN BY HIS WIFE, SONOKO, LED TO THE FAMILY'S REUNION AT POSTON CAMP IN ARIZONA.

Block 42, Building 7-D
Poston, Arizona
July 21, 1942

The Honorable Francis Biddle,
United States Attorney General
United States Department of Justice
Washington, District of Columbia

Sir:

I am taking this means to appeal to you for a reconsideration of the decision against Shigezo Iwata, my husband, who was taken into custody on March 11 from Carmel, California; given a hearing on May 16 at Santa Fe, New Mexico where he was detained; and transferred to Lordsburg, New Mexico on June 19 as an internee of war and now identified as ISN-75-4J-110-CI and located at Barrack 4, Camp 3, Company 9, Lordsburg Internment Camp.

I am an American citizen of Japanese descent and I believe in the government of the United States. I am grateful for the privileges I have been able to enjoy and share as a part of democratic America.

The decision you have recently rendered against Shigezo Iwata, my husband, must have been reached after a careful consideration but I am making this appeal to you in the hope that there might be room for reconsideration.

I solemnly affirm that Shigezo Iwata, my husband, has at all times been loyal to America and has always cooperated with our government, observing all regulations and trying his best to add constructively to the welfare of the nation. In the almost five years of our married life, I have always known

Poston, Arizona
July 21, 1942

The Honorable Francis Biddle,
United States Attorney General
United States Department of Justice
Washington, District of Columbia

Sir:

I am taking this means to appeal to you for a reconsideration of the decision against Shigezo Iwata, my husband. . . .

I am an American citizen of Japanese descent and I believe in the government of the United States. I am grateful for the privileges I have been able to enjoy and share as a part of democratic America. . . .

I solemnly affirm that Shigezo Iwata, my husband, has at all times been loyal to America and has always cooperated with our government, observing all regulations and trying his best to add constructively to the welfare of the nation. In the almost five years of our married life, I have always known him to practice simple honesty. He has been open-hearted, too, though markedly reserved. Our life has been a struggle on a small income but always there was hope and ambition for a higher living and we were slowly but surely attaining it. If Shigezo Iwata is returned to his family now settled at the Poston War Relocation Camp, I can assure you that he will cooperate and unite in efforts to build up this city of Poston which we know is a part of democratic America.

This appeal, I make, not because of our three small children who undoubtedly will receive more adequate care if their father could be with them nor for my own desire of keeping our family together since I know that countless number of homes are being permanently broken because of this conflict, but because I firmly believe Shigezo Iwata, my husband, is a loyal resident and has never been or never will be dangerous to the security of the United States. Moreover, to be considered as such is a dishonor we cannot bear to face.

Whatever your final decision, I shall still have faith in God and in our government but I keep praying that you will be able to give Shigezo Iwata a favorable decision.

Any word from you will be greatly appreciated.

Respectfully yours,
Sonoko U. Iwata
(Mrs. Shigezo Iwata)

Peter Ota was fifteen when his family was evacuated from Los Angeles. "We were put on a train," he says. "It was crowded. The shades were drawn. During the ride we were wondering, what are they going to do to us?" Days later the train arrived at "a desolate, flat, barren area. The barracks was all there was. There were no trees. . . . It was like a prison camp."

Peter and his family were among the more than 112,000 Japanese Americans imprisoned at ten internment camps hastily built in seven western states. The camps were set in dry, isolated areas and surrounded by barbed wire fences. Stretching as far as

MEMBERS OF A JAPANESE-AMERICAN FAMILY GATHER BEFORE THE HOME THEY WOULD BE FORCED TO EXCHANGE FOR A TINY BARRACKS IN A GRIM INTERNMENT CAMP.

A JAPANESE-AMERICAN WOMAN AND HER CHILD MAKE THEIR WAY TO AN INTERNMENT CAMP.

INTERNMENT CAMPS WERE SURROUNDED BY BARBED WIRE FENCES AND PATROLLED BY MILITARY GUARDS.

the eye could see were row after row of rough wooden barracks. racks. The barracks were divided into one-room "apartments," each furnished with cots, blankets, and a bare lightbulb. Families shared an apartment and ate in mess halls seating hundreds or even thousands. There was no indoor plumbing. "Every time I go to the bathroom at night," recalls Ben Segawa,

> I had to go to another building that was about fifty feet away. The minute I left our barracks, that searchlight would hit you and follow you right to where you were going. The light would wait there until you came back out . . . and followed you right back to your barracks again. They kept track of every move we made. I was only twelve years old, what could I do?

What the Japanese Americans did was make the best of things. "When people return to a state of nakedness, their true worth becomes evident," Hatsuye Egami, an interned mother of four, wrote in her diary. "I think that from this bare life we can weave something creative and interesting."

FOR INTERNED JAPANESE AMERICANS, MAIL EXCHANGED WITH FRIENDS ON THE WEST COAST WAS A LIFELINE TO THE OUTSIDE WORLD. IN THIS LETTER TO A FORMER TEACHER IN SAN FRANCISCO, SCHOOLGIRL ELSIE MIYATA DESCRIBES LIFE AT CALIFORNIA'S TANFORAN CENTER, A RACETRACK USED AS A TEMPORARY "ASSEMBLY CENTER" FOR PEOPLE AWAITING REMOVAL TO INTERNMENT CAMPS. ELSIE'S LETTER OUTLINES THE STEPS RESIDENTS TOOK TO CREATE A COMMUNITY WITH SCHOOLS, SERVICES, AND RECREATIONAL ACTIVITIES.

ELSIE'S SCENES FROM
LIFE IN TANFORAN

September 19, 1942

My Dear Miss Pitman,

September 28 will mark five months of camp life yet we may not be here to see it but in the short time we've been here many things have been done would you like to here some?

April 28, 1942—We arrived in Tanforan to find we were to live in a horse stable sleep in army beds and have stew six times a week.

May 8—We had our first visitors

9—First big dance in the social hall (11) First camp baby born a girl 7½ lbs.

15—First issue of the Tanforan news paper. 20—we ate in our own mess halls more important things in May

    4—library opened with 65 books later to be parlayed [increased] into several thousand

    25—The art school opened

    26—The school's opened and the music school was well on the way.

    The month of May was a hard one but July promised bigger things. On the 16th all people voted for his precincts. June too was the month of the beginning of sports & recreation. Talent shows began & the weekly Sat. dance followed by Tuesdays musicales

July—

    First and second pay checks were given. . . . On the 17th Tanforan opened her Golf course and the laundry & cleaning and barber shop. July was the month we put in our order for clothes supplied by the goverment.

August

    The 3rd & 8th—beginning of watch, radio, and shoe repairing services. 14th–15th The Wild West carnival given by rec. 9

    August 10th We had our first movie with Deanna Durbin in "Spring Parade". The movies were all free but money was accepted. In August too cupid played his part and Tanforan had her first marriage. At the month's end the people new they were leaving soon so once again we here the sound of the summer as the residents begin to take there home made furniture apart and crates for packing are made. We too have done something to help the war effort as every day we use thousands of cans Uncle Sam wants and he gets ours clean and pressed and we also had a rubber collection. So Miss Pitman this gives you a brief idea of what we can do but this work is only a sample as this is all temporarily built wait till we're all relocated and then things will begin to be built better & better and still with all the lovely things we have we all look forward to coming home and living again as before. . . . Inside are some drawings of the life in Tanforan. I really can't draw but—

    So Miss Pitman untill next time

Elsie

    P.S. Hope this letter hasn't bored you too much

Gradually the Japanese Americans transformed their barren camps into small towns complete with schools, libraries, hospitals, post offices, and police and fire departments. They held religious services and published newspapers. They organized orchestras, choirs, Boy Scout troops, and softball leagues. And they worked to bring beauty to their surroundings. Some planted trees, while others built furniture from scrap lumber, painted pictures, and sewed

INTERNED FAMILIES WORKED HARD TO BRING A TOUCH OF HOME TO THEIR DRAB NEW SURROUNDINGS.

curtains to make their drab apartments more homelike. In a letter to a friend back in San Diego, teenager Louise Ogawa described the efforts that went into making the 1942 New Year's Festival at Poston camp in Arizona bright and festive:

> *There were various exhibits. . . . Education was very interesting. There the work of the school children were displayed. Agriculture was another. In this building were many different kinds of vegetation. They were very green and looked as fresh as a daisy. The one I enjoyed most was the Arts and Craft. . . . Men have gone to cut mesquite trees and have made lovely flower vases out of them. The crooked branches and the bumpiest ones make the prettiest vases. In the vases there were many varieties of artificial flowers. . . . When we saw the rolls and rolls of beautiful artificial flowers—chrysanthemums—in a green house . . . it gave us a refreshing feeling.*

At the end of 1942, the government began freeing Japanese Americans who could prove they had a job waiting on the outside. Over the next two years, more than 34,000 people left the camps. These included some 8,000 young men who served in the armed forces, in segregated units that earned distinction for bravery in combat overseas.

Finally, in early 1945, the camps were closed completely. By that time many people were afraid to rejoin the hostile world outside the barbed wire fences. Those who returned to the West Coast often found their homes vandalized and businesses bankrupt. In all, Japanese Americans had suffered income and property losses of nearly a half billion dollars. In 1988 the U.S. government repaid a portion of those losses, issuing a formal apology for the "grave injustice . . . done to both citizens and permanent residents of Japanese ancestry." Today many historians call the wartime internment of Japanese Americans one of the worst violations of civil liberties in U.S. history.

In 1942 a number of Japanese-American men were temporarily released from the internment camps to work on farms in the surrounding areas. In a letter to Clara Breed, children's librarian at the San Diego Public Library, Louise Ogawa at Poston Camp described the hostility these workers encountered. Their experiences were one reason many Japanese Americans were reluctant to return to the outside world.

November 30, 1942

Dear Miss Breed,

. . . The boys who went out to work on the sugar beets in Colorado came home just in time to enjoy the Thanksgiving dinner with their families. All the boys who went out to work . . . are all back home now in good health. . . .

A friend who returned from Colorado related the following incident to me. He said, while in town a few boys entered a restaurant to have a bite to eat. The first thing the waitress asked was "Are you Japs?" When they replied "yes" she turned her back on them and said they don't serve Japs. So they had to go to another restaurant to eat. Here is another incident which disgusted the boys. When the boys asked a policeman where a certain store was he replied—"I don't serve Japs." One of the boys became angry and remarked—"Alright be that way—what do you think we came out here for? We didn't come to be made fun of—we came to help out in this labor shortage." Then the policeman apologized and showed them to the store. This boy said he certainly was glad to return to camp where there is no unfriendliness. Of course, he knows and we all know that there are people all over the world who hate certain races and they just can't help it. But I am sure when this war is over there will be no ratical [racial] discrimination and we won't have to doubt for a minute the great principles of democracy. . . .

Most sincerely,
Louise Ogawa

A WHITE MOB THREATENS A LONE BLACK MAN DURING THE 1943 DETROIT RACE RIOT.

Birth of the Civil Rights Movement

On a steamy night in June 1943, in a Detroit park where thousands had gathered to escape the heat, fistfights broke out between white and black teenagers. The fighting quickly swelled to a citywide riot. Mobs of young black men roamed the streets, smashing store windows and assaulting whites who strayed into the area. White mobs pulled blacks off streetcars and out of theaters and beat them. Over the next two days, thirty-four people were killed and hundreds injured. Finally, Michigan's governor called for federal troops, and an uneasy quiet was restored.

The Detroit riot and similar clashes in other U.S. cities that summer were a sign of the racial conflicts infecting the nation. Millions of Americans had migrated in search of work at defense plants and shipyards. Blacks, as they always had, found most doors shut tight. More than half of the new defense jobs were reserved for "whites only." Even when they found work, African Americans were restricted to lower-level jobs. "The Negro," according to one aircraft plant's written policy, "will be considered only as janitors and in other similar capacities. Regardless of their training as aircraft workers, we will not employ them."

Discrimination was common in the armed forces, too. African Americans could not enlist in the Air Corps or Marine Corps, and in the army and navy they were assigned to all-black units, where they trained as cooks, servants, and laborers. Black GIs from the north often got their first taste of rigid discrimination in communities near southern training camps. There they had to sit at the back of segregated buses and steer clear of "whites only" drinking fountains, movie houses, and lunch counters. "They want to send me 10,000 miles away to fight for democracy," one African-American GI complained, "when a hundred feet away they've got stools I can't put my black butt on and drink a bottle of beer."

In an attempt to protect the civil liberties of African Americans, President Roosevelt issued Executive Order 8802. It outlawed discrimination in hiring by government agencies and defense plants. That order, along with the growing need for defense workers, gave African Americans a foothold in industry. One million black Americans found jobs during the war, and the number of skilled black workers doubled as African Americans began entering trades that were previously all white.

"I started out pushing a broom," says James Majors, who went to work at a Chicago defense factory in 1943. James quickly worked his way up from janitor to drill press operator to machinist. "I was making just about as much money as any production

A. PHILIP RANDOLPH, THE FIERY HEAD OF AMERICA'S FIRST SUCCESSFUL BLACK LABOR UNION, REALIZED THAT GOVERNMENT LEADERS WOULD "NEVER GIVE THE NEGRO JUSTICE UNTIL THEY SEE MASSES . . . ON THE WHITE HOUSE LAWN." IN 1941 RANDOLPH WARNED PRESIDENT ROOSEVELT THAT, UNLESS ACTION WAS TAKEN, AFRICAN AMERICANS WOULD DESCEND ON THE CAPITAL IN A GIANT MARCH ON WASHINGTON. JOSEPH RAUH, WHO WORKED FOR WAYNE COY, SPECIAL ASSISTANT TO THE PRESIDENT, DESCRIBES THE PANIC—AND ACTION—THAT FOLLOWED.

A. PHILIP RANDOLPH LED THE FIGHT FOR EQUAL OPPORTUNITIES FOR AFRICAN AMERICANS IN EMPLOYMENT AND THE MILITARY DURING WORLD WAR II.

I got a call from my boss, Wayne Coy: "Get . . . over here, we got a problem." I must've run ten blocks. I come in all out of breath and Coy says, "Some guy named Randolph is going to march on Washington unless we put out a fair employment practices order. Do you know how to write an executive order?" I said, "Sure, any idiot can write an executive order, but what do you want me to say?" He said, "All I know is the President says you gotta stop Randolph from marching." "What's it all about?" He says, "We got defense factories goin' up all over this———country, but no blacks are bein' hired. Go down to the Budget Bureau and work something out."

By the next morning, we had a draft executive order saying that if you were a government contractor you had to nondiscriminate. We wrote this ———thing in about eighteen hours. I'm half dead, and Coy calls up: "It's not strong enough." . . . We try again, strengthen it a bit. Same thing: Randolph says it isn't strong enough. I thought, Who is this [guy]? Later, I became his lawyer. He had scared the government half to death. Finally, he did agree. It was issued as Order 8802. This was the first real executive blow for civil rights.

A Mixed Experience

While Japanese Americans were interned in camps and blacks struggled to be recognized as full-fledged members of society, Americans of German and Italian heritage had a very different wartime experience. They were white-skinned and strong in number. There were almost five million Italian Americans in the United States, including enough registered voters to concern politicians. Government leaders who supported Japanese-American internment called for more tolerant treatment of Italian immigrants. On Columbus Day 1942 the president responded by removing these noncitizens from the ranks of enemy aliens. While there were scattered cases of prejudice against Italian and German Americans during the war years, on the whole these groups escaped the wave of racial fear and hatred that engulfed people of Japanese heritage.

For other ethnic groups that had long suffered discrimination, the war was a mixed and confusing experience. Hispanic Americans dreamed of sharing in the nation's new prosperity and took pride in their race's contributions to the war effort. Mexican-American GIs played a major role in the liberation of the Philippines under General Douglas MacArthur, and Mexican laborers worked hard in California shipyards and western farm fields. Still, many businesses hung out signs announcing, "No Mexicans Hired," and police in Los Angeles looked the other way when white sailors beat up Mexican-American teenagers they considered juvenile delinquents. Hispanic children such as Diana Bernal of San Antonio, Texas, wrestled with the question of "why the Japanese Americans were placed in camps" and worried, "Are they going to do the same to us because we are Mexican?"

worker could. . . . The good part about it was that I was the only black, except for one other." William Barber was another trailblazer in an all-white field. As one of Philadelphia's first black streetcar operators, William was often insulted and even spit on by white passengers. "The biggest reason I continued," he explains, "was the principle of it. I figured that by doing that I would become somewhat like a pioneer. . . . And by breaking the ice I would make a better opportunity for the blacks to continue to be hired."

When Philadelphia began hiring black streetcar operators,

white drivers went on strike; it took eight thousand armed soldiers to end their protest. White workers in other cities also resented the gains blacks were making. They felt threatened by the competition for jobs and housing. Some feared that blacks introduced to prosperity would "rebel" and try to "take over." For their part, African Americans were frustrated by the agonizingly slow pace of change. Despite some small progress the armed forces remained largely segregated. The best jobs in industry and government were still reserved for whites. And in the housing crunch, blacks again bore the greatest burden, with many forced to live in overcrowded

AFTER WHITE STREETCAR OPERATORS WENT ON STRIKE IN PHILADELPHIA TO PROTEST THE HIRING OF AFRICAN AMERICANS, PRESIDENT ROOSEVELT SENT IN TROOPS TO KEEP THE CARS ROLLING.

Anti-Semitism at Home

It was one of the great contradictions of World War II. As Americans united in the fight against Nazism—the system raining terror and death on Jews in Europe—anti-Semitism (hostility toward Jews) on the homefront remained strong. American Jews faced discrimination in jobs and housing. They were often accused of draft dodging and of raking in unfair profits from the war. One girl who grew up in Pennsylvania was taunted by neighborhood boys who "rubbed thumb and fingers as I walked by and sneered, 'Money-money-money-money.'" When ten-year-old Philip Roth vacationed with his family on the New Jersey shore in 1943, he was terrorized by gangs of boys who "stampeded along the boardwalk . . . , hollering 'Kikes! Dirty Jews!' and beating up whoever hadn't run for cover." Roth, who would later become a famous novelist, found these attacks not only frightening but mystifying, "since we were all supposed to be pulling together to beat the Axis Powers."

ghettos. All these frustrations and tensions between the races exploded in the riots that shook Detroit and other industrial cities.

World War II ended with a solution to these problems far from sight. But the seeds of change had been planted. Some of the barriers against African Americans in employment and in the military had been broken. Black civilians and GIs who had enjoyed greater opportunities during the war years were more dissatisfied than ever with inequalities in jobs, housing, education, and other areas. "A wind *is* rising," wrote Walter White, president of the NAACP (National Association for the Advancement of Colored People), "a wind of determination by the havenots of the world to share the benefits of freedom and prosperity which the haves of the world have tried to keep exclusively for themselves." Over the next decade that wind would build into the hurricane known as the civil rights movement.

SHORTAGES AND SACRIFICES

There was a large vacant lot and everybody got together and had a gigantic communal [shared] victory garden. My sister and I thought it was a wonderful place to go, because it was like Alice in Wonderland to get out there on a Saturday morning and all the neighbors were watering their squash and their green beans. They'd give things away to everybody. Nobody said, This is mine. Everything was upbeat.

—SHERIL CUNNING, LONG BEACH, CALIFORNIA

Volunteers for Victory

Despite racial conflicts, nearly all Americans were united in one common goal: to win the war. World War II was the only war in the twentieth century overwhelmingly supported by the American people. It was "the good guys versus the bad guys," remembers James Covert, who was nine years old when his father and older brother enlisted. "It was very clear in everybody's mind who was right and who was wrong."

It was clear, too, that every American had a part to play in the war effort. "This war offers us stay-at-homes a greater chance for real service than any war in the past," said one enthusiastic civil defense worker. More than twelve million Americans volunteered at their local Office of Civilian Defense. They trained as plane

IN A MOCK AIR RAID, CIVIL DEFENSE VOLUNTEERS PRACTICE CARING FOR "VICTIMS" OF AN ENEMY ATTACK.

spotters, air-raid wardens, ambulance drivers, bomb-defusing crews—all sorts of jobs intended to protect the population in case of air attack. During air-raid drills, civil defense volunteers might toss flames to imitate bombs while others scurried about giving "first aid" to Boy Scouts doused with ketchup. When communities practiced nighttime blackouts, air-raid wardens patrolled the streets, making sure no light peeked through a window to guide enemy bombers.

"Something I'll always remember about the war were the air raids . . . and how strictly they were enforced," says Paul Kneeland, who worked as a reporter for a Boston newspaper.

There was a tie-up on the streetcar line one night. . . . Six or seven streetcars were stalled, automobiles were honking their horns, flashing their lights. And the air-raid warning sounded. . . . Immediately all the streetcars on the line turned out their lights. All the automobiles, maybe 150 on Main Street, turned out their lights, and there was total silence for half an hour. . . . It was as though they expected that within ten minutes a bomb was going to drop.

After 1942 fears of enemy bombings faded. Still, civil defense workers and other volunteers continued their efforts in homefront campaigns to help ensure victory. Some rolled bandages for the Red Cross or volunteered at hospitals that were short on nurses. Some worked at USO (United Service Organizations) centers, which were set up to offer GIs a hot meal and recreational activities. Nearly everyone found time to plant a "victory garden."

Soon after the war began, government leaders, knowing there would be food shortages, began to encourage people to grow their own vegetables. Gardens began springing up everywhere— in tiny backyards and vacant lots, at gas stations and on city rooftops. There was even a large community plot at a racetrack in Chicago and one at the zoo in Portland, Oregon. By 1943 Americans had planted some twenty million victory gardens, producing more than a third of all the vegetables grown in the country.

Not all home gardens were a complete success. Sheril Cunning of Long Beach, California, describes her family's first try at a vegetable patch as "the most miserable, hard-as-cement, three-by-five-foot plot of ground. . . . [We] grew radishes and carrots as our contribution to the war. But radishes weren't anybody's mainstay, and our carrots never got bigger than an inch." Even a puny harvest couldn't dampen the determined victory gardener's enthusiasm. "We all wanted to do our part for the war," Sheril explains. "You got caught up in the mesmerizing [hypnotic] spirit of patriotism."

Scrap drives offered another chance to pull together for the

SERVICEMEN AND CIVILIANS
GATHER IN NEW YORK CITY'S
TIMES SQUARE FOR THE
DEDICATION OF A GIANT CASH
REGISTER BUILT TO PROMOTE
THE SALE OF WAR BONDS.

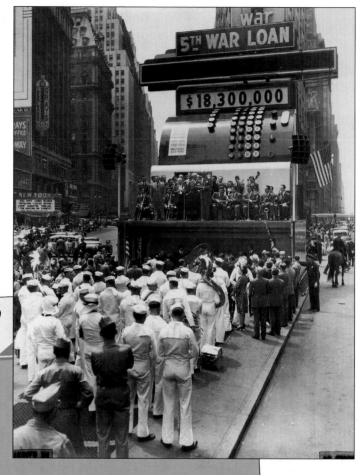

"Back the Attack!"

In New York City's Times Square, a four-story-tall cash register kept a running total of money raised for the war effort through the sale of war bonds. The bonds were issued by the U.S. government. Individuals and corporations could buy them in amounts ranging from $25 to $10,000 and cash them in later for the purchase price plus interest. Altogether, Americans bought about $135 billion in bonds during the war years.

War bonds were sold just about everywhere—at banks, post offices, movie theaters, food stores, and booths at church picnics and county fairs. Through giant rallies complete with costumes, comedy, and song, Hollywood stars sold millions of dollars' worth of bonds. Even superheroes did their part. In comic strips and comic books, Batman and Superman urged their readers to buy bonds and "Back the Attack!"

common good. Metals, rubber, and other materials critically needed by defense factories were in short supply. Americans met the
crisis with a great nationwide scavenger hunt. They brought millions of old tin cans, razor blades, lipstick tubes, toy trucks, pots
and pans, and car fenders to collection centers for recycling into
planes, tanks, ships, guns, and ammunition. Rubber boots, garden
hoses, and hot-water bottles became new tires and tank treads.
Nylon made tow ropes. Silk stockings were reborn as parachutes.
Patriotic homemakers even saved their kitchen fats. Fat contains

A HOMEFRONT BOY—ONE OF THE MILLIONS OF CHILDREN WHO LENT A HELPING HAND
IN SCRAP DRIVES—PREPARES TIN CANS FOR RECYCLING INTO WAR MATERIALS.

glycerin, a compound used to make explosives; according to a government bulletin, one pound of fat had enough glycerin to make one pound of black explosive powder. So women strained their used cooking fat, bacon grease, and meat drippings, and brought the filled cans to their butchers. Their reward: two food ration points and the satisfaction of taking one more step toward victory.

CHILDREN WERE AMONG THE NATION'S MOST ENTHUSIASTIC SUPPORTERS OF HOME-FRONT VICTORY CAMPAIGNS. IN A LETTER TO GENERAL DOUGLAS MACARTHUR, COMMANDER OF ALLIED FORCES IN THE SOUTHWEST PACIFIC, TWELVE-YEAR-OLD JOAN DOOLEY DESCRIBED SOME OF THE WAYS SHE AND HER FRIENDS WERE CONTRIBUTING TO THE WAR EFFORT.

Wichita, Kansas
Nov. 10, 1942

Dear Sir:

You may wonder why I am writing and who I am. Well to begin with I saw a piece in the paper that said a little boy of nine wrote to you. That gave me the same idea, so that is why I am writing to you. You may want to know what I look like so I will try my best to describe myself. I am twelve and about 5 foot 1 in. I have brown eyes and brown hair. I am in the seventh grade at school and I like all of my teachers, which is quite unusual. I supposed you would like to know what we at home are doing. My mother saves grease for bullets. I also buy a war stamp every time I get a quarter. We save paper, all kinds of metal and rubber. I have a bicycle but I don't very often ride it to save rubber tires. One of the milk company's has organized a club for children called, "The Juniour Commandos," and they are doing a great job. We Girl Scouts are doing our bit by taking care of small children so that the parents may work in war factories. We are also running errands for people. . . . Well it is about time for taps so I had better be closing this letter.

Yours Truely
Miss Joan Dooley

Homefront Melodies

The music of World War II swelled with strong emotions: patriotism, love, loneliness, loss. Here are titles of some of the popular songs that fed Americans' fighting spirit and helped express the feelings of those at war and those they left behind.

"Praise the Lord and Pass the Ammunition"
"Boogie-Woogie Bugle Boy (of Company B)"
"Der Fuehrer's Face"
"Rosie the Riveter (B-r-r-r-r-r! B-r-r-r-r-r!)"
"Scrap Your Fat"
"Any Bonds Today?"
"It's Been a Long, Long Time"
"When the Lights Go On Again (All Over the World)"
"I'll Be Home for Christmas (If Only in My Dreams)"

"Use It Up, Wear It Out"

While Americans cheerfully lent a hand to scrap drives and other voluntary activities, they did grumble about two troublesome features of homefront life: shortages and rationing.

Shortages of consumer goods began soon after Pearl Harbor. Some items, such as rubber, silk, and sugar, were no longer being shipped from parts of the world embroiled in war. Others, such as wool and tin, were needed to make uniforms and canned foods for GIs. Still others included common household products labeled "nonessential to the war effort." Factories that had been making toothpaste tubes, coat hangers, toasters, refrigerators, bicycles, and hundreds of other "nonessentials" began turning out war materials instead.

In May 1942 the government came up with a system to make sure everyone got their fair share of scarce goods. Every man, woman, and child was issued a series of ration books. The books contained sheets of tiny color-coded stamps. In order to buy rationed goods, a consumer had to tear out the correct number of stamps and give them to the merchant along with the purchase price. To further complicate matters, stamps were only good for a certain period of time, and the number needed to buy different items frequently changed. A pound of hamburger meat might cost five points today, seven points tomorrow. Foods covered by rationing included everything from sugar, coffee, and meat to ketchup, baby food, cheddar cheese, and canned sardines.

A SHIPMENT OF MEAT BRINGS CROWDS TO THE BUTCHER SHOP, EAGER TO EXCHANGE THEIR RATION STAMPS FOR A RARE TREAT.

WHEN THE GOVERNMENT ANNOUNCED THAT MEAT WOULD BE ADDED TO THE LIST OF RATIONED FOODS, CONSUMERS MOBBED BUTCHER SHOPS, SNAGGING EVERY LAST STEAK AND CHOP. WRITING FROM MILWAUKEE, WISCONSIN, DOLORES "DEE" SAMPON DESCRIBED THE PANIC BUYING TO HER FIANCÉ, J. DONALD PEEL. PEEL WAS A SERGEANT WITH THE FIFTH ARMY, NINTH DIVISION, STATIONED IN AFRICA. DOLORES WROTE HIM EVERY DAY FROM THE BEGINNING OF THEIR SEPARATION IN APRIL 1942 UNTIL HIS RETURN IN OCTOBER 1945.

Saturday, March 27 [1943]

Darling, I've heard about it and read about it—but yesterday I actually saw the crowds of people waiting to be able to get inside a meat market. Why some of them must have stood hours. This shop in particular was advertising meat loaf—no limit—they surely laid themselves wide open. Everything is being held back until after tomorrow when the rationing goes into effect. We have been quite fortunate—Thursday I was able to get corned beef and made the natural combination corned beef and cabbage. . . . That was the only kind of meat again today but I couldn't repeat it that soon so we had a Spanish omelet for supper— and never missed the meat. Sausage is still available so tomorrow we have grilled wieners rolled in bacon strips. I'm not trying to make you hungry, dearest. . . . But what I was driving at was that all the talk, all the distracted buying is really a mild form of hysteria, isn't it? After all it isn't necessary— there are so many things that can be prepared in its place—it seems just the idea of coming rationing and probably the very sound of the word that acts like a spur to stock up—and the way some do buy—their amounts are surely going to be long spoiled before they are able to use it all. Isn't it a funny business, darling? . . .

I am your
Dee

Just as complicated was the system for gas rationing. All motorists received a windshield sticker with a letter from *A* to *E,* based on how the family car was used and how much gas its owner was entitled to buy. Those who used their cars for errands got the least gas, commuters got a little more, and emergency workers such as police officers and firefighters could buy all they needed. Other goods were rationed according to a variety of different formulas. Consumers were limited to two pairs of shoes per year. They could buy waterproof boots and other rubber products only if they could prove they had special war-related needs. The amount of fuel oil allowed depended on the size of the home and the number of small children living there.

FARMERS, WHOSE WORK WAS CONSIDERED ESSENTIAL TO THE WAR EFFORT, USUALLY RECEIVED AS MUCH FUEL OIL AS THEY NEEDED. HOWEVER, THE MOUNTAINS OF PAPERWORK THEY HAD TO FILL OUT OFTEN RESULTED IN AGGRAVATION AND DELAYS. IN A LETTER TO HIS LOCAL RATIONING BOARD IN DUNKIRK, NEW YORK, ONE INDIGNANT FARMER, WHOSE NAME IS NOT KNOWN, ENCLOSED A BILL TO COVER LOSSES CAUSED BY A DELAYED SHIPMENT OF KEROSENE.

Dear Miss———

We received no certificate so we could buy kerosene for a stove to warm a house in which to keep little pigs. The pigs were born last night; they are all dead. Enclosed you will find a bill to cover the loss. We hope and pray you may influence the board to grant us our request for kerosene to keep the house warm for the other sow who will have her pigs during that week.

We are sorry your board was delayed in their acting on this, for it means eight pigs that will not be raised to help win the war. Please act as soon as possible.

Yours truly

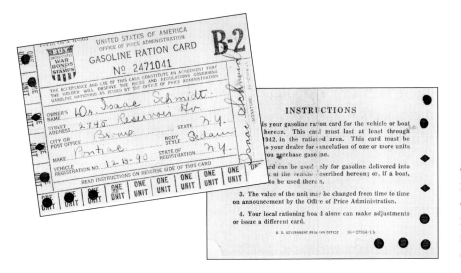

GAS RATIONING PUT AN END TO LEISURELY SUNDAY DRIVES; THE OWNER OF THIS CARD HAD TO LIMIT HIS DRIVING TO MAKE SURE HE DIDN'T USE UP ALL HIS GASOLINE CREDITS.

Everyone complained about rationing. "For the life of me I don't see why they don't put more stamps in those books," wrote Phil Haughey from Portland, Oregon. "They keep us running for some form of rationing every month."

Phil's wife, Frances, had another concern. "Fuel rationing for Oregon starts tomorrow," she noted in a January 1943 letter, "and as our building is oil heated . . . we expect to shiver from now on."

As the war progressed, many people *did* shiver. During the chilly winter of 1942–1943, consumers were allowed barely enough rationed oil to heat homes to 65°F. Even goods that were not rationed became harder and harder to find. Chewing gum, cigarettes, laundry soap, tissues, thumbtacks, bobby pins, needles, buttons, and thousands of other everyday items were scarce and sometimes disappeared altogether. Frustrated consumers had no choice but to follow the government's advice: "Use It Up, Wear It Out, Make It Do, or Do Without."

"My grandfather was something of a genius in repairing tires that were no good," recalls John E. Smith of Soldotna, Alaska. "I remember people coming over at night with an old damaged tire asking Grandpa to please fix it, and he would." Most tires were driven until they were bald. Junkyards were scavenged for spare parts to repair broken-down automobiles. To save their cars and gas rations, people began riding in car pools or on crowded streetcars and buses. Homemakers spent their evenings patching the family's old clothes. Some women even used needle and thread to repair runs in stockings; when their last pair was gone, they switched to socks or covered their legs with makeup.

Mealtime presented special challenges. Americans drank less coffee, with less sugar. They scraped the barest dab of butter on toast or used a new substitute called oleomargarine—a creamy white spread that looked something like butter after a powdered dye was stirred in. "I know you heard of eggless, milkless butterless

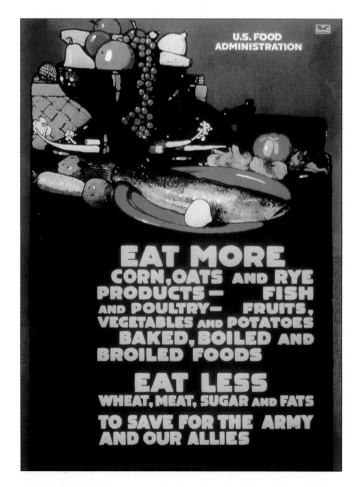

DURING THE WAR YEARS, THE U.S. GOVERNMENT CREATED NEARLY 200,000 DIFFERENT POSTERS, MANY DESIGNED TO INSPIRE HOMEFRONT AMERICANS TO SUPPORT PROGRAMS SUCH AS FOOD CONSERVATION AND RATIONING.

cakes," wrote a Pennsylvania woman sending a food package to a friend overseas, "but mine is sugarless too. (just a warning) ha-ha." For cooks tired of making do with fish, pasta, and vegetable casseroles, butchers began selling horse meat, buffalo, and antelope steaks. *Gourmet* magazine approved the trend toward creative cooking with this holiday jingle:

> *Although it isn't*
> *Our usual habit,*
> *This year we're eating*
> *The Easter Rabbit.*

Despite all their grumbling, people managed to cope with wartime shortages. Most grudgingly agreed that the rationing system was basically fair. For homefront Americans, coping with daily frustrations and inconveniences was just one more contribution to the war effort.

5

ON TO VICTORY

Did you know my father Lt. George Gilbert Soper he was in Manila.
He was at General Hdq. Phillippine Dept and was assistant adjutant.
If so will you please tell me if he was wound or killed. If you find
him when you go back to the Phillippines will you tell him that we
have a baby bother named for him. He is one 1/2 years old.

—ELVA RUTH SOPER, AGE ELEVEN,
TO GENERAL DOUGLAS MACARTHUR, APRIL 1943

Absent Fathers

All across the nation families waited. As the long war dragged on, the parents, brothers and sisters, wives and sweethearts of American GIs longed for good news and dreaded the bad. "There was just that kind of hurt," says Almira Bondelid, describing the years her husband served overseas, "an ache inside that must be there when someone in the family dies. . . . I could be laughing and talking to friends, and the ache would be right there." All through the war Almira's father-in-law "took piano lessons just to keep his mind occupied. The day my husband came home for good, he stopped."

No one was more affected by the pain and uncertainties of wartime separations than children. Along with the increase in marriages, war had brought a sharp rise in the birth rate. From 1941 through 1945 nearly 15 million babies were born in the

Hasten the Homecoming

BUY VICTORY BONDS

United States. Many lived their first few months or years without a father. Older children watched their fathers leave home to face danger and possibly death. Sheril Cunning, who was seven when war was declared, remembers one friend who worried about her father, serving with the Coast Guard. "We would always look at letters from her father. It was a house with a woman and child growing up all those years alone and living on letters. I think Nora's father was killed. Shirley Somebody's father was away. We talked about it at school all the time. Absent fathers."

REUBEN BERMAN SERVED AS AN ARMY PHYSICIAN IN EUROPE FROM JUNE 1943 TO SEPTEMBER 1945. DURING HIS ABSENCE, HIS WIFE, ISABEL, HELPED THEIR THREE OLDER CHILDREN—DAVID (AGE NINE IN 1943), BETSY (SIX), AND SAMMY (FOUR)—KEEP IN TOUCH WITH THEIR FATHER THROUGH LETTERS. THE CHILDREN'S LETTERS DISCUSSED THE WAR, THEIR HOMEFRONT CONTRIBUTIONS, SCHOOL, PLAY, AND THEIR LOVE AND CONCERN FOR THEIR FATHER.

June 7, 1944
Dear Poppy:

I hope you don't get killed in the invasion. If you come back and spank me I will have the right to make you feel badder than anything and tell you that you are not like Abraham Lincoln so you had better not come back and spank me. . . .

The paper sale is not to be tooken to school. It is to be put out on the boulevard and the paper is tooken away. And I hope you're nice yet. But I don't want you to be kind to the Germans or Japanese because they're mean. . . .

I've got a poem for you. "Hirohito, I hope you choke when Tokyo goes up in smoke." I hope the Germans are killed in that invasion. You might not be killed but you might be wounded. I hope you're not shot because if you're shot I'll feel very bad because I would like to have a poppa, you same poppa, that same poppa. . . .

Sammy

FOUR-YEAR-OLD SAMMY BERMAN DESCRIBED THIS DRAWING SENT TO HIS FATHER, REUBEN, AS "A SHIP AND A JAP PLANE THAT THE SHIP SHOT DOWN. . . . THE SHIP SHOT DOWN THE PLANE AND THERE IS A PICTURE OF THE PILOT BAILING OUT."

September 20, 1944

    Dear papa,

    I weigh fifty pounds.

    School starte sept 6th.

    If i had wings like a angel I would take some bombs and fli over to germany and japen and bom them. Then you could come home sooner. I want you most if all.

    When sammy said that you were just like abraham lincoln he was right. . .

                               Love, Betsy

May 6, 1945

    Dear Papa:

    At long last we have had victory over the would be destroyers of mankind. For 6 years the Nazis oppressed humanity in ways which have never been exceeded in the history of the earth. But now I want to get to the point. I believe that now that we have won victory over the Nazis, you and other men should be allowed to come back home again. I think that there are many people who would agree with me on that.

    I am glad you are sending Betsy a flute because I think that will suit her very nicely. But what will we do with the violin from the Goldsteins?

    Have you seen any of the prison camps? Please for God's sake Don't.

                               Love, David

Even though no battles were fought on U.S. soil, the war was very real to homefront children. Their school days began with the Pledge of Allegiance and a prayer for all Americans in the armed services. They staged patriotic school plays, sang patriotic songs, and joined in Victory Assemblies, flag raisings, and parades. In the school lot and at home, they played war games. A backyard or nearby woods might become Germany or the South Pacific, where junior GIs armed with wooden rifles dodged "hand grenades" and dived for "foxholes." Many children spent hours making model fighter planes and studying news accounts of the fighting. "I got all the airplane magazines and books I could afford," says one former homefront boy from Chicago, "and could identify anything that flew."

Junior Commandos

Children also channeled their fierce patriotism into tremendous contributions to the war effort. They worked in victory gardens, knit socks and mittens for GIs overseas, and gathered the pods of milkweed plants, which were used as stuffing for life preservers. Each day at school they plunked down their hard-earned change to buy ten- and twenty-five-cent defense stamps. The stamps were pasted into savings booklets; when full, the booklets could be exchanged for a twenty-five-dollar war bond. In 1944 alone stamps and bonds bought by schoolchildren paid for nearly 3,000 military planes, 44,000 jeeps, and 12,000 parachutes.

Children's efforts really stood out in scrap drives. Ransacking their homes and neighborhoods, youngsters collected mountains of cans, tin foil, paper, and other recyclables. In St. Louis a schoolgirl who went from door to door dragging two wooden wagons won a city award for collecting 1,220 pounds of scrap in one week. The Boy Scouts collected a grand total of 502 million pounds of scrap rubber and metal during the war years. One of their paper drives was so successful it had to be shut down after they hauled in more than the paper mills could handle.

Many young people joined special wartime youth groups, such as the Junior Service Corps and Little Orphan Annie's Junior Commandos, whose members collected scrap, sold war stamps and bonds, and played war games. Children performed small, private patriotic services, too. Seven-year-old Michael McCall of

A LOS ANGELES, CALIFORNIA, "JUNIOR COMMANDO" UNIT SHOWS OFF ITS GROWING PILE OF USED TIRES, COLLECTED IN ANSWER TO PRESIDENT ROOSEVELT'S CALL FOR A NATIONWIDE SCRAP RUBBER DRIVE.

Kansas donated his prized red-and-white pedal car "to win the war." The boy swelled with pride when his car was placed atop his school's twenty-foot pile of scrap. In Maplewood, New Jersey, two young teenage boys circled their neighborhood after a heavy snow-fall, shoveling the front walk of every house with a service flag in the window—a sign that a family member was in the service. The boys rang no bells and took no payment; after clearing fourteen walks, they went home, exhausted.

"There was such a unity of spirit that hardly anyone questioned any war-winning effort," recalls a man who grew up in Alabama. Children reveled in this sense of wartime unity and in the knowledge that their actions contributed to the nation's victory. "Everyone was patriotic to their very being," wrote a homefront girl from Newark, Ohio. "Everyone sacrificed and worked for one cause—America and to keep our freedom."

The Final Push

On June 6, 1944, the Allies invaded Normandy, France. D-Day—the launch of the final Allied campaign against the Axis—had finally come. Battling fierce resistance, troops pushed across German-occupied Europe, liberating town after town. The home-front watched anxiously. Victory was near, but casualties were mounting—more Americans would die in the last year of the war than in the first three and a half years combined.

AMERICANS GREETED THE NEWS OF THE D-DAY INVASION WITH MIXED EMOTIONS—JOY THAT VICTORY IN EUROPE WAS NEAR, ANXIETY FOR THE TENS OF THOUSANDS OF ALLIED TROOPS WHO FACED DEADLY RESISTANCE FROM NEARLY OVERWHELMING GERMAN FORCES. BARBARA SANZ OF VALPARAISO, INDIANA, DESCRIBED HER FEELINGS IN A LETTER TO LESTER "MAC" MCCLANNEN, A WARTIME PEN PAL WHO WOULD BECOME HER HUSBAND AFTER HIS RETURN IN JULY 1945.

Valparaiso, June 6, 1944

Dear Mac,

Now I understand why I have not heard from you. The "Day" has come. I can't explain the feeling I had when I first heard of the Invasion. I heard it when I walked in the shop this morning. I was stunned. We all knew it was coming and were happy that it is started, so it can all end soon. When it actually happens it's a shock. It was such a gloomy day, rained all day. That didn't help much. We had the radio going all day. The President gave a prayer tonite that the nation was to join. Believe me, when I say I put my whole heart and soul in that prayer and will continue to pray knowing that you and the other boys have help and come out on top. And as for you especially, Mac, do take care of yourself. I am still anxiously waiting to meet you and will keep on waiting. . . .

God Bless You, Barbara

April 1945 brought shock and grief at the death of President Franklin D. Roosevelt. FDR had led the nation out of the depths of the Great Depression. His optimism, energetic leadership, and the reassuring sound of his voice during his radio "fireside chats" had sustained Americans through the long war years. Early in April 1945 the president, sick and weary after meetings in Europe with other world leaders, visited a resort in Warm Springs, Georgia, where he often sought relief from the polio that had left his legs paralyzed. On April 12 he died of a brain hemorrhage.

CROWDS SHOW THEIR SORROW AS THE FUNERAL PROCESSION OF PRESIDENT FRANKLIN D. ROOSEVELT PASSES THROUGH THE STREETS OF WASHINGTON, D.C.

The news struck Americans like the death of a family member. People crowded the streets, shocked and sobbing. "It doesn't seem possible," said one Detroit woman. "It seems to me that he will be back on the radio tomorrow, reassuring us that it was just a mistake." Children felt sad and frightened. "He was president when I was born and I was almost 12 when he died," recalls one former homefront boy. A girl from Dover, Delaware, "was shocked the day we learned that President Roosevelt had died. I had assumed that he would be president forever."

I N THIS LETTER TO A GI SERVING IN CHINA, A YOUNG WOMAN FROM WASHINGTON, D.C., EXPRESSED THE NATION'S SORROW AT THE LOSS OF PRESIDENT FRANKLIN D. ROOSEVELT.

April 17, 1945

Hi, Lt. [Lieutenant],

. . . This past week-end was a very sad one here in Washington—as it was all over the nation. President Roosevelt's death was such a tragic thing and such a shock. It seems impossible even now—I've never been conscious of any other President and like so many other people, I imagine, I more or less took him for granted. Before the war, he was seen around Washington quite often and he would always be in an open car. During the summer nearly every week end he would go on cruises down the Potomac. So many Sunday afternoons I've seen him coming back up Penn. Avenue, waving at people and smiling. [This] Saturday morning [his body] was brought back to Washington from Georgia and on my way to work I passed Union Station. His train was due at 10:00 and people were already gathering when I went past. I couldn't help remembering other times he's come into the Station and a crowd would be waiting. He was truly a great man. . . .

Yours,
Ruth

A month after Roosevelt's death, Germany surrendered. Americans celebrated V-E (Victory in Europe) Day. Still the war in the Pacific raged on. The death toll climbed as American forces captured island after island from fierce Japanese defenders who fought to the death. Experts predicted that years of hard fighting lay ahead, with many more American lives sacrificed. All that changed on August 6, 1945.

AFTER FDR'S DEATH, HARRY S. TRUMAN BECAME PESIDENT. HERE, WITH HIS WIFE, BESS, AND DAUGHTER, MARGARET, BY HIS SIDE, HARRY S. TRUMAN TAKES THE OATH OF OFFICE AS THE THIRTY-THIRD U.S. PRESIDENT.

"It was in the evening that we received the news," recalls James Covert of Portland, Oregon.

I walked out on the back porch, and my mother was sitting on the steps crying. I sat down next to her and I said, "Mother, the war is almost over. You don't have to cry anymore. My brother and Dad will be home." But she said, "I'm crying because I think we may have done something we are going to be sorry for."

The United States had dropped a horrific new weapon, the atomic bomb, on the Japanese city of Hiroshima. Four square miles of the city were instantly evaporated and 100,000 people killed. Three days later a second bomb was dropped on Nagasaki, killing or wounding 75,000. On August 14 Japan surrendered. World War II was over.

KAY MCREYNOLDS WAS A STUDENT AT THE UNIVERSITY OF MISSOURI WHEN NEWS CAME THAT THE WAR WAS OVER. SHE DESCRIBED HER FEELINGS IN A LETTER TO HER FIANCÉ, JIM MCKEMY, A NAVY SUPPLY OFFICER STATIONED IN THE SOUTH PACIFIC. JIM WOULD RETURN HOME ON DECEMBER 26, 1945, AND THE COUPLE WOULD MARRY THREE WEEKS LATER.

Trenton, Aug. 14, 1945

Dearest Jim:

. . . It's going to be quite an adjustment, this peace stuff. I can't even remember a time that we weren't in a war or preparing for one, or at least talking about it. But I must add that it's an adjustment I'll make with relish.

The [radio] announcer is saying that it is expected that President Truman will make an announcement any time. . . . Honestly, the suspense is almost unbearable. No doubt you are the same way. We are hearing about the reactions of the men in the Pacific. . . .

This is the most wonderful day of my life! I know you and the others have this same feeling, only multiplied. I feel awfully proud right now, and rather humbled. So many men, including some of our friends, have given their lives just for this day. . . . The fire siren and [factory] whistle have been blowing and a train whistle, too. We're all crying, even Daddy. Mama just said that she has felt that way only once before, when I was born. Just think, you'll be coming home to stay! And, maybe our children will never have to know what war is. . . .

Good does *triumph over evil! How can we civilians ever repay the armed services? Yes, I feel most humble. . . .*

I love you, Kay

Coming Home

Joy and tears, riotous celebrations, quiet thanksgiving—Americans greeted the news of the war's end with an explosion of emotions kept bottled up inside for years.

"I've never seen anything like it," wrote a young Michigan woman. "Uptown Ann Arbor is a riot, streamers, confetti, papers flying through the air. . . . Policemen on every corner but they've decided long ago [not] to try and keep order. They're just leaning on lamp posts and letting the people do what they will." The scene was the same in cities throughout the nation. Crowds jammed the streets, dancing and shouting, laughing and crying, welcoming V-J (Victory over Japan) Day at the top of their lungs.

YOUNG AND OLD, SERVICEMEN AND CIVILIANS—AMERICANS KICKED UP THEIR HEELS AND REJOICED AT THE END OF WORLD WAR II.

The celebration, says one San Francisco woman, "was like being in the middle of the wildest, craziest carnival you'll ever see in your whole life."

For many Americans, V-J Day was a time for quiet reflection. Seven-year-old Connie Amaro heard bells ringing in her small Texas town and "saw people in our neighborhood running out of their houses to the church to Thank God." Jill Oppenheim de Grazia in Chicago noted, "I haven't felt at all like celebrating." Uncertain when her GI husband would return from Europe, Jill wrote gloomily, "The only people who could go out and howl tonight are those totally disinterested in the war." For some, the merriment stirred painful memories. "There were shouts of joy, dancing in the streets," says Vicki Lacount, who was seven years old when her father died in Belgium at the Battle of the Bulge. "I was not rejoicing. The war never ended for me because my Dad never came home."

EVERY GI'S FAMILY LIVED IN FEAR OF THE KNOCK ON THE DOOR THAT MIGHT BRING A TELEGRAM WITH THE DREADFUL WORDS, "REGRET TO INFORM YOU . . ." KNOWING LITTLE ABOUT THE LAST MOMENTS OF A LOVED ONE'S LIFE OFTEN ADDED TO A FAMILY'S GRIEF. IN THIS LETTER TO THE COMMANDING OFFICER OF HER BROTHER'S MARINE CORPS REGIMENT, A YOUNG WOMAN SEEKS ANSWERS TO QUESTIONS TORMENTING HER HEARTBROKEN FAMILY.

Stromsburg Nebr.
July 19 1945
John P. Stone
1st Lt., U.S.M.C.R.,
Commanding
Co. "I" 3rd Bn. 29th Mar. Regt.

Dear Mr. Stone:

Your letter of June 27 to Thorn Shinn, concerning the death of Ralph Shinn was received July 16.

It was very much appreciated and we take this means of thanking you.

I am Ralph's youngest sister. There were 4 of we girls and Ralph. We all thought he was very special and worshiped even the ground he trod upon.

Altho all we have left is our memories of him they are good. He was always a good boy and very thoughtful.

Mother and father are heartbroken but have somehow found comfort in God's Word and courage to carry on. But they just don't feel like writing.

We [realize] he was only one of many in your command and probaby there were others who fell with him. But there was so little in the papers about the 6th Marines and he was never allowed to write much. We surely would appreciate it if you could possibly find time to write us again and give us more details.

Maybe we are funny folks but we feel if we could only know the whole truth just how and all, it would maybe help end this awful nightmare.

Were there any of his buddies left. Could you ask them to write to us?

What about the chaplain—wasn't there one when he was laid away. Couldn't he write to us.

Your letter was all that has been received about it.

We understand that Ralph's division was on patrol duty on northern Okinawa.

When did you enter into the fight on Southern Okinawa? Where was it *at—Naha—Asa River—Sugar Loaf Hill? When was it—morning noon or night? Was he alone, didn't anyone hear his last words, what they were or was it too quick even for that.*

How was he laid away. Was there coffins or burlap or were they just laid on the bare ground. What about the cemetery? What is it like where is it, North or South Okinawa?

We will be eternally grateful to you if you can write and answer our questions and tell us anything more in regards to it.

We are praying to God to help you and keep you safe to carry on and finish it.

Thanking you again for your letter and hoping to hear from you again I will close now.

Respectfully yours
Mrs. N. P. Hansen
Stromsburg Nebr.

In the months that followed the war's end, millions of GIs came home. They and their families tried to pick up the pieces of their old lives. Many found it difficult. The nation and its people had changed. Some felt bitter, resenting the years "wasted in war" and yet missing the lost sense of purpose, of working together for a common cause. As the devastation caused by the atomic bomb became known, some began to question its use. "We didn't drop those two on military installations," says Victor Tolley, who had cheered the bombings until a Marine Corps assignment took him to Nagasaki. "We dropped them on women and children. The very minute I was jumping up and down and hugging my buddy . . . there was a little baby layin' out in the street charred and burned and didn't have a chance to live."

All Americans hoped that the terrible new weapon need never be used again. And above all, they prayed that the end of war would bring a lasting peace. "Somehow we've got to unscramble enough eggs to make a Sensible World," urged novelist Booth Tarkington, "an Anti-Killing World—and a 'Land of Liberty.'" Tucking in her sleeping child, one young mother reflected, "I was gazing on the face of one individual who probably won't see another war." But others were less optimistic and, sadly, closer to the truth. "I still refuse to believe," wrote Bertha Peel from Geneva, New York, "that there is going to be a chance in a million that . . . the lion and the lamb will be able to lie down together in peace and friendship. Human nature has not changed since the beginning, so the lamb better look out."

CONCLUSION: A NEW WORLD

World War II was the most destructive war in history. No one knows for sure how many died, but estimates put the number at 40 million or more, including 6 million Jews murdered during the Nazi Holocaust. American casualties totaled more than 290,000 killed in action and 670,000 wounded.

For millions of people around the world, the war meant air raids, invasions, terror, and destruction. The United States was spared all that. Still, the war changed American life and society forever.

GIs returned to a land where millions of people had moved to new homes, especially in the cities and the west. It was a land of big business and big dreams. Companies that had grown rich churning out tanks and planes were now mass-producing cars, TV sets, and refrigerators. After years of the Great Depression and wartime shortages, Americans whose pockets bulged with wartime wages were eager to buy. And thanks to the GI Bill, a congressional act passed in 1944, veterans were able to join the widespread prosperity. Through benefits and loans the GI Bill enabled World War II veterans to go to college or job-training schools, buy their own homes, and start new businesses.

Along with the postwar prosperity came new products and technologies. Most had been developed for military needs; these included synthetic (artificial) rubber, new kinds of plastics, improved computers, radar, and life-saving penicillin. Homebuilders brought their new knowledge of mass production to the suburbs, where row after row of new houses multiplied, each just like its neighbor. Another by-product of war was "big government." The complex network of government agencies created during the war now influenced nearly every aspect of the nation's life. Most

IN THE PROSPEROUS POSTWAR YEARS, MILLIONS OF AMERICANS SETTLED IN THE NEW SUBURBAN HOUSING DEVELOPMENTS SPRINGING UP ACROSS THE NATION.

Americans had gotten used to looking to their government for guidance and were happy to continue. All were proud to belong to the nation that had emerged from war as the richest and strongest power in the world.

There was a downside to the postwar boom, however. As veterans returned to the workforce, the women who had taken their places in offices and factories suddenly found themselves unemployed. Whether they liked it or not, women were expected to resume their traditional roles as full-time wives and mothers. Black Americans, too, found the doors that had been opened during the war years shut tight again. But the self-image and expectations of women and blacks had changed. Women who returned to their homes or settled for lower-paying jobs passed their dreams down to daughters and granddaughters, who grew up believing they could be anything they wanted to be. African Americans and other minorities, proud of their wartime accomplishments, fought with increasing success to expand on the gains they had made. World War II had changed the face of America—and planted seeds of change that would bear fruit for future generations.

TIME LINE OF WORLD WAR II EVENTS

1939	1940	1941	1942

1942

- **January 1** Twenty-six Allied nations sign the Declaration of the United Nations, pledging to fight the Axis forces.
- **January 6** American and Filipino forces in the Philippines, commanded by General Douglas MacArthur, begin a retreat to the Bataan Peninsula.
- **March 21** The evacuation of Japanese Americans to internment camps begins.
- **April–May** Rationing of sugar, gasoline, and other consumer goods begins in the United States.
- **April 9** U.S. forces in Bataan surrender to the Japanese.
- **May 4–8** Battle of the Coral Sea: American air and naval forces defeat a Japanese invasion fleet.
- **May 14** The Women's Army Auxiliary Corps (WAACs), the first women's military unit in the United States, is created.
- **June** The mass murder of Jews begins in the gas chambers of Auschwitz concentration camp in Poland.
- **June 4–6** Battle of Midway: American aircraft sink four Japanese aircraft carriers in the central Pacific.
- **August 7** U.S. forces land on Guadalcanal, in the southwest Pacific.

1940

- **April 9** Germany invades Norway and Denmark.
- **May 10** Germany invades France, the Netherlands, Belgium, and Luxembourg.
- **June 10** Italy declares war on Great Britain and France.
- **June 14** German troops enter Paris.
- **September 16** Roosevelt establishes the first compulsory (nonvoluntary) peacetime draft in the United States.
- **September 27** Germany, Italy, and Japan unite forces by signing the Tripartite Pact.

1939

- **September 1** Germany invades Poland.
- **September 3** Great Britain, France, Australia, and New Zealand declare war on Germany.
- **September 5** President Franklin D. Roosevelt proclaims the United States neutral.

1941

- **December 7** Japan bombs the U.S. naval base at Pearl Harbor, Hawaii.
- **December 8** The United States declares war on Japan.

1943

● **February 2** German troops surrender at Stalingrad, Russia— the first major defeat of Hitler's armies.

● **July 9–10** The Allies land in Sicily.

● **September 3** Italy surrenders to the Allies.

1944

● **January 10** Congress passes the GI Bill of Rights, to aid returning servicemen and servicewomen.

● **June 4** Allied forces enter Rome, Italy.
● **June 6** D-Day invasion: The Allies invade Normandy, France.

● **August 25** German forces in Paris surrender.

● **September 13** The Allies cross the border into Germany.

● **October 20** American forces under General Douglas MacArthur return to the Philippines.

● **November 7** Roosevelt is elected U.S. president for the fourth time.

● **December 16** Battle of the Bulge: German troops fight American forces in the Ardennes.
● **December 18** The U.S. Supreme Court rules that loyal American citizens cannot be held in detention camps against their will—the first step toward closing the Japanese-American internment camps.

1945

● **February 19** U.S. forces land on Iwo Jima, off the coast of Japan.

● **March 7** The Allies open a pathway into the heart of Germany.

● **April 1** U.S. forces invade the Japanese island of Okinawa.
● **April 12** President Franklin D. Roosevelt dies; Vice President Harry S. Truman succeeds him.
● **April 25** Soviet troops surround Berlin, Germany.
● **April 30** Adolf Hitler commits suicide in an underground bunker in Berlin.
● **May 7** Germany surrenders to the Allies.
● **May 8** V-E (Victory in Europe) Day is celebrated.

● **June 26** The United Nations Charter is signed by representatives of fifty Allied nations.

● **August 6** The United States drops an atomic bomb on Hiroshima, Japan.
● **August 9** The United States drops a second atomic bomb on Nagasaki, Japan.
● **August 14** Japan surrenders, ending World War II.

GLOSSARY

Allies The nations united against the Axis powers in World War II. The Allies included the United States, Great Britain, Russia, and more than thirty other nations.

anti-Semitism Hostility toward Jews.

arsenal A place used for the manufacturing or storage of arms and other military equipment.

Axis powers The three powers—Germany, Italy, and Japan—that fought against the Allies during World War II.

blitzkrieg A war conducted with great speed and force; in German, "lightning war."

civil defense A system of protections conducted by civilians during an attack or a natural disaster.

draftsman A person who draws plans and sketches for ships, buildings, and other construction projects.

emancipated Freed from bondage.

evacuation The process of removing people from a military zone or dangerous area.

Fascism A political system that puts the good of the state above the rights of the individual. Fascist governments are headed by a dictator who allows no opposition to government policies and controls.

GI Bill The Servicemen's Readjustment Act of 1944, a congressional act that provided World War II veterans with tuition for college or vocational school, as well as low-interest loans for home buying and new businesses.

hemorrhage A large, rapid release of blood from the blood vessels.

internment camps Guarded camps where more than 112,000 people of Japanese descent were imprisoned during World War II.

Issei (EE-say) Japanese immigrants to the United States.

migrant A person who moves from place to place, usually in search of work.

Nazi A member of the National Socialist German Workers' Party, led by Adolf Hitler from 1920 to 1945. The Nazis believed in government by dictatorship, anti-Semitism, and the racial superiority of Germany's white "Aryan" race.

non-com A noncommissioned officer, or lower-ranking officer in the army, air force, or marines.

PX "Post exchange"; usually a store at a military base where GIs and their families can shop and get their mail.

rationing A system used to make sure that all people get their fair share of essential items, such as food or gasoline, that are in short supply.

Rosie the Riveter An imaginary person featured in government ad campaigns to encourage women to work in war factories.

TO FIND OUT MORE

Books and Periodicals

Gay, Kathlyn, and Martin Gay. *World War II*. Voices from the Past series. New York: Twenty-First Century Books, 1995.
Easy-to-read account of key events in the war, with some information on the homefront; includes first-person perspectives by people on all sides of the conflict.

Harris, Jacqueline. *The Tuskegee Airmen: Black Heroes of World War II*. Parsippany, NJ: Dillon Press, 1996.
Story of the pioneering African-American aviators who battled prejudice to become fighter pilots during World War II.

Harris, Mark Jonathan, Franklin Mitchell, and Steven Schechter. *The Homefront: America During World War II*. New York: G. P. Putnam's, 1984.
Chronicles conditions and changes on the homefront through interviews with ordinary Americans whose lives were changed by war; written in conjunction with the PBS documentary "The Homefront."

Houston, Jeanne Wakatsuki, and James D. Houston. *Farewell to Manzanar*. Boston: Houghton Mifflin, 1973.
Memoir of a young girl's experiences in a Japanese-American internment camp; sad, funny, and fascinating.

Isserman, Maurice. *World War II*. New York: Facts on File, 1991.
Good, detailed resource on the objectives, strategies, key battles, weapons, and impact of the war.

Stein, R. Conrad. *The Home Front*. Chicago: Children's Press, 1986.
Brief, easy-to-read overview of life on the homefront, with lots of good black-and-white photographs.

On the Internet*

"Dear Miss Breed: Letters from Camp" at
http://www.lausd.k12.ca.us/janm/breed/title.htm
A "virtual exhibition" of letters, oral histories, photographs, and home movies relating to Japanese-American children held at internment camps, from the collection of the Japanese American National Museum.

"Further and Further Away: The Relocation of San Diego's Nikkei
    Community, 1942." *The Journal of San Diego History*,
    Winter–Spring 1993, at http://sandiegohistory.org/journal/
    spring93/chapter1.htm
On-line edition of The Journal of San Diego History, *published by the San
Diego Historical Society. This issue focuses on the experiences of Japanese
Americans evacuated from San Diego and includes letters, poems, oral histo-
ries, and photographs.*

"Ginger's Diary" at http://www.art-bzl.com/diary.html
*On-line diary of a seventeen-year-old girl who lived at Hickam Field, near
Pearl Harbor, at the time of the Japanese bombing on December 7, 1941.*

"The History Place: World War Two in Europe" at
    http://www.historyplace.com/worldwar2/timeline/ww2time.htm
*Time line of key events of World War II in Europe, with links to photographs
and in-depth text.*

"Powers of Persuasion: Poster Art from World War II" at
    http://www.nara.gov/exhall/powers/powers.html
*Thirty-three colorful World War II posters, selected from an exhibit in the
National Archives Building in Washington, D.C. Sound files play excerpts from
songs and speeches.*

"War Relocation Authority Camps in Arizona, 1942–1946" at
    http://www.library.arizona.edu/wracamps/
*An exhibit of photographs taken for the federal government's War Relocation
Authority camps, depicting life in Arizona's two Japanese-American intern-
ment camps.*

"What Did You Do in the War Grandma?" at
    http://www.stg.brown.edu/projects/WWII_Women/intro.html
*Twenty-six Rhode Island women talk about their experiences during World
War II, in interviews with ninth graders as part of an English class project;
includes glossary, time line, and links to other World War II sites.*

**Websites change from time to time. For additional on-line information, check with the media
  specialist at your local library.*

BIBLIOGRAPHY

Asbell, Bernard. *Mother & Daughter: The Letters of Eleanor & Anna Roosevelt*. New York: Coward, McCann & Geoghegan, 1982.

Bailey, Ronald H., and the editors of Time-Life Books. *The Home Front: U.S.A.* Alexandria, VA: Time-Life Books, 1978.

Berman, Ruth, comp. *Dear Poppa: The World War II Berman Family Letters*. Edited by Judy Barrett Litoff. St. Paul: Minnesota Historical Society Press, 1997.

Blum, John Morton. *V Was for Victory: Politics and American Culture During World War II*. New York: Harcourt Brace Jovanovich, 1976.

Brinkley, Douglas. "A Tale of War & Remembrance." *New York Daily News*, January 2, 2000, pp. 32–33.

Brokaw, Tom. *The Greatest Generation Speaks: Letters and Reflections*. New York: Random House, 1999.

Calvocoressi, Peter, Guy Wint, and John Pritchard. *Total War: Causes and Courses of the Second World War*. New York: Pantheon Books, 1989.

Clawson, Augusta M. *Shipyard Diary of a Woman Welder*. New York: Penguin, 1944.

Egami, Hatsuye. *The Evacuation Diary of Hatsuye Egami*. Edited by Claire Gorfinkel. Pasadena, CA: Intentional Productions, 1995.

"Further and Further Away: The Relocation of San Diego's Nikkei Community, 1942." *The Journal of San Diego History*, Winter–Spring 1993. http://sandiegohistory.org/journal/spring93/chapter1.htm

Harris, Mark Jonathan, Franklin Mitchell, and Steven Schechter. *The Homefront: America During World War II*. New York: G. P. Putnam's, 1984.

Hartmann, Susan M. *The Home Front and Beyond: American Women in the 1940s*. Boston: Twayne, 1982.

Heide, Robert, and John Gilman. *Home Front America: Popular Culture of the World War II Era*. San Francisco: Chronicle Books, 1995.

Heiferman, Ronald. *World War II*. London: Octopus Books, 1973.

Hoehling, A. A. *Home Front, U.S.A.* New York: Thomas Y. Crowell, 1966.

Honey, Maureen. *Creating Rosie the Riveter: Class, Gender, and Propaganda During World War II.* Amherst, MA: University of Massachusetts Press, 1984.

Hoopes, Roy. *Americans Remember the Home Front.* New York: Hawthorn, 1977.

Isserman, Maurice. *World War II.* New York: Facts on File, 1991.

Lingeman, Richard R. *Don't You Know There's a War On? The American Home Front, 1941–1945.* New York: G. P. Putnam's, 1970.

Litoff, Judy Barrett, and David C. Smith. *Since You Went Away: World War II Letters from American Women on the Home Front.* New York: Oxford University Press, 1991.

Litoff, Judy Barrett, David C. Smith, Barbara Wooddall Taylor, and Charles E. Taylor. *Miss You: The World War II Letters of Barbara Wooddall Taylor and Charles E. Taylor.* Athens, GA: University of Georgia Press, 1990.

Polenberg, Richard. *War and Society: The United States, 1941–1945.* New York: J. B. Lippincott, 1972.

Rogers, Donald I. *Since You Went Away.* New Rochelle, NY: Arlington House, 1973.

Satterfield, Archie. *The Home Front: An Oral History of the War Years in America, 1941–1945.* New York: Playboy Press, 1981.

Snyder, Louis L. *The War: A Concise History 1939–1945.* New York: Julian Messner, 1960.

Taylor, A. J. P. *The Second World War: An Illustrated History.* New York: Paragon Books, 1975.

Terkel, Studs. *"The Good War": An Oral History of World War Two.* New York: Pantheon, 1984.

Tuttle, William M., Jr. *"Daddy's Gone to War": The Second World War in the Lives of America's Children.* New York: Oxford University Press, 1993.

Winkler, Allan M. *Home Front U.S.A.: America During World War II.* Arlington Heights, IL: Harlan Davidson, 1986.

Wright, Michael, ed. *The World at Arms: The Reader's Digest Illustrated History of World War II.* London: Reader's Digest Association, 1989.

NOTES ON QUOTES

The quotations in this book are from the following sources:

Chapter One: Arsenal of Democracy
p. 12, "First it was indignation": Harris, Mitchell, and Schechter, *Homefront*, p. 26.
p. 14, "great arsenal": Winkler, *Home Front U.S.A.*, p. 5.
p. 14, "speed and speed now": ibid.
p. 15, "After all those years": Satterfield, *Home Front*, p. 171.
p. 17, "an immediate change": Winkler, *Home Front U.S.A.*, p. 17.
p. 19, "We didn't fly": Terkel, *"Good War,"* pp. 118–119.
p. 19, "I was *always* the new kid": Tuttle, *"Daddy's Gone,"* p. 55.
p. 20, "I need a lot of mail": Litoff et al., *Miss You*, p. 199.
p. 20, "Letters were a big part": Harris, Mitchell, and Schechter, *Homefront*, p. 198.
p. 23, "Before the bomber plant": Polenberg, *War and Society*, p. 142.
p. 23, "You never got the feeling": Terkel, *"Good War,"* p. 119.
p. 23, "Folks in houses": Polenberg, *War and Society*, p. 143.

Chapter Two: Rosie the Riveter
p. 24, "Suddenly I saw something": Terkel, *"Good War,"* p. 135.
p. 24, "If you can drive": Bailey, *Home Front*, p. 86.
p. 24, "When the war started": Harris, Mitchell, and Schechter, *Homefront*, pp. 128–129.
p. 28, "We Can Do It," ibid., p. 116.
p. 30, "it took . . . two weeks": ibid., p. 126.
p. 30, "The men said" and "Leaving my . . . daughter": ibid., pp. 132–133.
p. 30, "Goddam it all" and "Why can't these gals": Bailey, *Home Front*, p. 55.
p. 32, "stumbling into": Tuttle, *"Daddy's Gone,"* p. 70.
p. 32, "It was . . . a very hectic": Harris, Mitchell, and Schechter, *Homefront*, p. 171.
p. 34, "there were many": ibid., p. 175.
p. 34, "Georgie keeps my busy": Litoff and Smith, *Since You Went Away*, pp. 86–88.
p. 34, "I lived alone": Harris, Mitchell, and Schechter, *Homefront*, p. 191.

Chapter Three: Democracy Denied
p. 36, "Open season": Bailey, *Home Front*, p. 26.
p. 36, "No Dogs": Tuttle, *"Daddy's Gone,"* p. 171.
p. 37, "free shaves": Blum, *V Was for Victory*, p. 158.
p. 40, "We were put": Terkel, *"Good War,"* pp. 29–30.
p. 41, "Every time I had": "Further and Further Away," p. 12.
p. 41, "When people return": Egami, *Evacuation Diary*, pp. 27–28.
p. 45, "There were various exhibits": Louise Ogawa to Clara Breed, January 6, 1943, Japanese American National Museum.
p. 45, "grave injustice": Civil Liberties Act of 1988, at http://www.children-of-the-camps.org/history/civilact.html
p. 48, "The Negro": Polenberg, *War and Society*, p. 114.
p. 48, "They want to send me": Bailey, *Home Front*, p. 55.
p. 49, "never give the Negro": Polenberg, *War and Society*, p. 102.

p. 48, "I started out": Hoopes, *Americans Remember*, p. 95.

p. 50, "why the Japanese Americans": Tuttle, *"Daddy's Gone,"* p. 167.

p. 50, "The biggest reason": Harris, Mitchell, and Schechter, *Homefront*, p. 104.

p. 52, "rubbed thumb" and "stampeded along": Tuttle, *"Daddy's Gone,"* pp. 185, 184.

p. 52, "A wind *is* rising": Winkler, *Home Front U.S.A.*, p. 66.

Chapter Four: Shortages and Sacrifices

p. 53, "There was a large": Terkel, *"Good War,"* p. 238.

p. 53, "the good guys": Harris, Mitchell, and Schechter, *Homefront*, p. 86.

p. 53, "This war offers": Polenberg, *War and Society*, p. 132.

p. 54, "Something I'll always remember": Hoopes, *Americans Remember*, pp. 288–289.

p. 55, "the most miserable": Harris, Mitchell, and Schechter, *Homefront*, p. 70.

p. 63, "For the life" and "Fuel rationing": Phil Haughey letters, February 22, 1943, and January 31, 1943: Haughey Family Papers, Bentley Historical Library, The University of Michigan.

p. 63, "Use It Up": National Archives and Records Administration, at http://www.nara.gov/exhall/powers/waste.html

p. 63, "My grandfather": Brokaw, *Greatest Generation Speaks*, p. 207.

p. 64, "I know you heard": the Lees to Herbert G. Raab, February 26, 1942: Raab Family Collection, U.S. Army Military History Institute.

p. 65, "Although it isn't": Satterfield, *Home Front*, p. 199.

Chapter Five: On to Victory

p. 66, "Did you know": Elva Ruth Soper to Douglas MacArthur, April 1943, MacArthur Memorial Archives and Library.

p. 66, "There was just": Satterfield, *Home Front*, p. 113.

p. 67, "We would always look": Terkel, *"Good War,"* p. 236.

p. 70, "I got all": Tuttle, *"Daddy's Gone,"* p. 141.

p. 71, "to win the war": ibid., p. 124.

p. 71, "There was such" and "Everyone was patriotic": ibid., pp. 127, 132–133.

p. 73, "It doesn't seem possible": Bailey, *Home Front*, p. 202.

p. 73, "He was president" and "was shocked": Tuttle, *"Daddy's Gone,"* p. 131.

p. 75, "It was in the evening": Harris, Mitchell, and Schechter, *Homefront*, p. 210.

p. 77, "I've never seen anything": Litoff and Smith, *Since You Went Away*, p. 271.

p. 78, "was like being": Satterfield, *Home Front*, p. 366.

p. 78, "saw people": Tuttle, *"Daddy's Gone,"* p. 213.

p. 78, "I haven't felt": *Grazian Archive* at http://www.grazian-archive.com/let45auga.htm

p. 78, "There were shouts": Tuttle, *"Daddy's Gone,"* p. 215.

p. 80, "We didn't drop": Terkel, *"Good War,"* p. 545.

p. 81, "Somehow we've got": Booth Tarkington to Margaret Booth Jameson, July 29, 1943: Booth Tarkington Papers Collection, Indiana Historical Society.

p. 81, "I was gazing": *Grazian Archive* at http://www.grazian-archive.com/let45auga.htm

p. 81, "I still refuse": Bertha M. Peel to Dolores Sampon, December 21, 1943: Sgt. J. Donald Peel Collection, 9th Infantry Division, 5th Army, Box 9, U.S. Army Military History Institute.

INDEX

Page numbers for illustrations are in **boldface**

ABOUT THE AUTHOR

"The hours I spent at libraries searching for the 'voices' of the LETTERS FROM THE HOMEFRONT series were filled with delightful discoveries: crayon notes from a kindergartner to his big brother serving in Vietnam, a cardboard box crammed with more than a thousand letters sent to a World War II serviceman in Europe by his devoted fiancée, golden locks of hair tucked inside the crumbling leather diary kept by a Pennsylvania woman during the Civil War. What struck me most was how familiar all these voices sounded. In times of trouble, it seems, people through the centuries have shared much the same doubts and fears, bitterness and heartache, love of family and country, humor, courage, dreams. I hope readers will be touched by the same sense of discovery and appreciation of the indomitable American spirit."

VIRGINIA SCHOMP has written dozens of books for young readers, including many published by Marshall Cavendish on subjects ranging from history to biography to careers. Ms. Schomp lives in New York's Catskill Mountains with her husband (and A-1 research assistant), Richard, and their son (and champion reader), Chip.